BE 12

BEst!,

Amy Maguire

BE 12

The Energy to Live Your Values

AMY R. MAGUIRE

XULON PRESS

Xulon Press
2301 Lucien Way #415
Maitland, FL 32751
407.339.4217
www.xulonpress.com

ISBN-13: 978-1-54565-938-0

TABLE OF CONTENTS

Note to Readers

Thank you for BElieving in me. It is an honor to join you on the path to BEing your BEst. I recognize there are countless motivation, self-help and devotional selections available. I have shelves full of them and am thankful to the authors whose wisdom guides me. This book has been on my heart for years. It began as a writing to myself, a way for me to BE a better person, a better; wife, mother, friend, daughter, sister. As I watched our daughters grow into wonderful young women, I was called to provide more values for their path. The more I interacted with other women, the more I found we face similar challenges as we strive to BE our best.

I believe BE 12 will refresh, refocus and reenergize you. I pray these words will leap off the pages to your mind and heart. These 12 values have helped me climb the mountain from deep valleys. They have given me strength to BE brave and have led me to a more focused, on-purpose life.

Dedication

To those who went before me and forever left their fingerprints on my heart. They each taught me how to live a value focused life. Mignon taught me character, culture and to be kind to all. Uncle Billy, whose calm spirit and zest for adventure made sure I knew anything was possible. Ruth was the mother-in-law that not only raised a loving, generous, dedicated son, but also taught me how to not sweat the small stuff. Daddy, the glass full, man of faith that never had a harsh word to say of anyone, instilled values of love and kindness.

Thank you to the amazing women who shared their values with me. Your actions, words, and deeds are the energy of BE 12. I am grateful for great gal pals that fill my vibrant village. Beth, Kim, Jules, Katja, Tiffany, Debbie, Jane, Sarah, and Laura. You make me BEtter. You have celebrated with and supported me through the pains and joys of life. Thank you for sharing your values.

And, to the fun, adventurous, loving family I am blessed to call mine. God has blessed me beyond measure. You give me energy and keep me grounded. There is no greater man than my husband, Sean. And our daughters, Megan and Molly, you are the wind beneath my wings. I am so proud of the women you are BEcoming. Your values continue to grace and bless me and all you touch.

BE 12

THE ENERGY TO LIVE
YOUR VALUES

THERE IS A PLACE IN TIME, WHERE WE BECOME
our BEst selves. You may be seeking that place right now.
That place is not an endless list of to-dos. It is not full of
negative self talk or comparing ourselves. It's a place where
you are your authentic self, living your values. Gal pals, we
need to stop doing and start BEing.

The busyness we call life trapped me to a threatening
point. On one sunny Florida day, I saw how my life might
end. It wasn't the ending I had planned. God has plans for
me and for you. Plans to prosper, to keep us from harm, and
for hope and a future.

Your personal value system consists of principles and
ideas. BE 12 is designed for you to think, reflect, and
grow. Each month is packed with values, principles, scripture, and prayer. The final week of the month is a chance
to reflect, recycle, and refresh your energy as you BEcome
your BEst self. And because I have seen the power of prayer,
each day you are encouraged to write your prayer. You will
see the "Godicles", miracles from God, that are delivered
when we pray.

Values became my compass as I focused on the true North. Let's travel together and learn more about ourselves and the woman God created us to be. May these words guide you to build, grow and live your values.

BE:

Authentic, Confident, Curious, Disciplined, Encouraging, Faithful, A Leader, Fun, On-Purpose, Respectful, Transformative And BE yourself.

BE 12 or B12

Values are critical to healthy living and B12 is essential for life. Without the vitamin B12, our brain and heart cannot function effectively and we may suffer from chronic fatigue.

Read more to see how this vitamin B12 will help your BE 12.:

Give you energy. The nutrient releases energy into the cell and provides you with the appropriate balance you need for thinking and moving throughout your day.

Keep you sharp. Researchers have found that patients with dementia and Alzheimer's disease have much lower levels of B12 than those of a similar age who have a sharp, clear memory.

Make your heart happy. B12 removes a dangerous protein called homocysteine from the blood. If homocysteine is allowed to roam through blood, it damages your arteries, leading to inflammation and heart disease.

Make your bones stronger. Studies have found patients with osteoporosis have lower levels of B12 than people with strong, healthy bones.

Protect your nerves. Myelin sheaths protect our nerves from toxins. B12 supports the way your body replenishes these nerve coverings.

Keep you smiling and looking good. B12 regulates your mood and has been found to give you more energy. Wear and tear as we age affects our DNA and slows its correct replication. B12 supports DNA health keeping our cells young and keeps us looking and feeling young.

Now, let's juice up on BE12! Give yourself time and space to BE. This book is created for you to BEtter know yourself and your values. We spend a lot of energy caring for others, climbing the ladder, comparing ourselves, or feel just plain too scared to know who we are and for what we stand. We have to take care of ourselves in order to BE our BEst. Find your happy spot and open yourself to BEcoming.

Introduction

Why Can't I Have an Aspirin?

On January 1, 2018, I developed a focused strategy to finish a book that I had dreamed about for years. I detailed the hours to write and research. The plan was designed to prioritize family while managing client needs, financial pressures, and relationships. Sister, I need to tell you, it was hard. I have so much respect and admiration for authors. Writing a book is not for the weak of heart. I knew BE 12 was critical to success. Running your own company, raising teenagers, being a wife and friend, and staying within our family budget required BEing centered and focused. The temptations to give up were frequent. Each time I was tempted to give in, a burning bush set ablaze in front of me and lit the path back. Whether it was a friend who needed to talk about their challenge with values or the epiphany of a stranger on the sidewalk, God led me to today.

The plan sailed smoothly like a boat toward a spectacular sunset. Then a crashing wave hit the bow, ready to sink the ship. It is the call you never want, and it came to me on Monday afternoon in February. My daughter and mother were in a car accident. This was one of two crashing waves God sent to say, "I will guide you to your BEst self."

The second wave, a near tsunami, arrived three months later as I was close to completing the book. On a beautiful Florida afternoon, I joined a group of female friends for a baseball game. My friend and mentee, Anita, and I left in deep conversation. Typically, we would have taken the stairs, but we took the elevator, which was one of many "Godicles" that day. The next thing I recall, I dropped my sunglasses, purse, and was unable to speak. Anita was able to get me to the ground outside the elevator and called for help. Unable to speak, my arms and legs tingled and I lost feeling. I was scared! I could hear words in my head but couldn't speak them. I saw the smiles my soul mate, Sean, our incredible daughters, and the many faces of family and friends. In my mind, I prayed loud to God. I am good at begging and bartering with God from my deepest valleys. My overwhelming fear was, had I lived a life worthy of BEING who God designed me to BE? How was I living my value system to serve?

In the ambulance, the young paramedic was calm and precise. My heart rate raced, the tingling continued, and he urged me to breathe slowly. One, two, three, four, five. . . five, four, three, two, one. I am a yogi, so surely, I got this! I was consumed with fear. While I have lived a great life, I was not ready for it to be over. Surely, there was more to my story. There were more people to love and serve. If given another chance, I vowed to share values and principles of living a life of service to God and others.

When I regained my speech, the first words I started barking were, "May I have an aspirin?" For many reasons, I always carried an aspirin in my purse. In addition to loved ones who relied on them for heart issues, I am a migraine survivor, and aspirin is the "fix." So, bossy, "control enthusiast" Amy was large and in charge.

"May I have an aspirin? Why can't I have an aspirin?" Well, of course, the medical personnel were smarter than me and the right protocol was to assess the problem before they gave a solution. But my controlling, bossy self jumped into overdrive. "Assess the problem before fixing it" was not my style.

Upon arriving in the Emergency Room, God had assembled a collection of experienced and caring physicians, nurses, medical professionals, friends, and family. I wish I could spend these pages telling you about the friends that supported me, and how Tiffany, John, and Katja rushed to the hospital. Carol and many friends waited in the lobby and others reached out in prayer and support. Seeing how others showed up was humbling. And, of course, my soul mate, the spectacular, one-of-a-kind, loyal, solid, husband, Sean, was there every minute.

For many months, I was poked, prodded and underwent many tests and procedures. Was it a stroke, a seizure, a nervous breakdown, clot, blockage, or maybe B12 deficiency? We still do not have the answers, nor do we know if it will happen again, so I refer to it as my "spell." Only God knows if I will live twenty-five more years or twenty-five more minutes. I don't know what tomorrow holds, but I know *who* holds tomorrow. I know now a life worth living is not measured by length, but by depth.

Twelve Isn't Just
Any Number

THE JOURNEY TO BEcome your BEst is a monumental commitment from you. Deciding to focus on your values and BEcoming your BEst is not for the weak of heart. We know the vitamin B12 gives us energy, keeps our hearts happy and our brains sharp. But what is special about this number twelve and its significance? As I reflect on personal and professional growth, twelve has represented many milestones. Those include the first year of; marriage, new job, parenting, exercise regime, or writing a book. For me, dedicating time every day for twelve months was my first step on BEcoming BEtter. I hope you find these facts refreshing as you think about the time you need for personal and professional growth.

- Twelve is derived from four threes. Three is the sign of the Trinity: Father, Son, and Holy Ghost.
- The smallest perfect number is six. Six times two is twelve.
- The number of space and time.
- Apollo 12: the second manned spacecraft to land on the moon on November 14, 1969.
- Twelve men have walked on the moon.
- Twelve is the number of months in a year.

- Twelve is the symbol of completeness and perfection.
- Revelation 12:1: "And great portent appeared in heaven, a woman clothed with the sun, with the moon under her feet and on her head a crown of twelve stars."
- My husband and I were both born on the twelfth day of a month, six months apart.

Twelve Days of Christmas

Folklore or not, this song dates back to the 1700s during a period of religious persecution. It was written as a catechism song to worship without fear of persecution. I hope you find the meanings symbolic.

- One partridge in a pear tree: Jesus Christ.
- Two turtle doves: the Old Testament and the New Testament.
- Three French hens: faith, hope, and love.
- Four calling birds: the four Gospels in the New Testament: Matthew, Mark, Luke, and John.
- Five golden rings: the first five books of the Old Testament, also known as the Hebrew Torah or the Pentateuch, which are Genesis, Exodus, Leviticus, Numbers, and Deuteronomy.
- Six geese-a-laying: the six days of creation.
- Seven swans-a-swimming: seven gifts of the Holy Spirit found in Romans 12:6-8: prophecy, serving, teaching, exhortation, generosity, leading, mercy/compassion.
- Eight maids-a-milking: eight Beatitudes found in Matthew 5:3-10: "Blessed are the poor in spirit, those who mourn, the meek, those who hunger and thirst for righteousness, the merciful, the pure in heart, the peacemakers, and those who are persecuted for righteousness sake."
- Nine ladies dancing: nine fruits of the Spirit from Galatians 5:22-23: love, joy, peace, patience, kindness, goodness, faithfulness, gentleness, and self-control.

- Ten lords a-leaping: The Ten Commandments.
- Eleven pipers piping: eleven faithful Apostles: Simon, whom He named Peter; Andrew; James, John, Phillip, Bartholomew, Matthew, Thomas, James, Simon and Judas.
- Twelve drummers drumming: symbolizes the twelve points of the Apostles' Creed.

And there is more.

- Twelve sons of Jacob who were the patriarchs of the twelve Tribes of Israel.
- Twelve Judges were those that God raised up in the Old Testament to keep the people in check.
- Twelve disciples: Peter, Andrew, James, John, Philip, Bartholomew, Thomas, Matthew, James, Simon, Judas, and Judas Iscariot.
- Twelve stones described in Joshua 4 directing Joshua to choose twelve men, one from each tribe.
- Twelve stones were placed in the water which allowed the Israelites to carry the Ark of the Covenant across the Jordan River.
- Twelve loaves of bread were left after Jesus fed the 5,000 as described in Matthew 14:13-21.
- Jewish girls are Bat Mitzvah at twelve and Jewish boys are Bar Mitzvah at twelve.
- The twelve stones on the breast piece at the Tabernacle as described in Exodus 28:15-21. The breastplate of Aaron is described in great detail with a different

gemstone listed for each of the twelve tribes of Israel. The stones are: carnelian, chrysolite, emerald, turquoise, sapphire, amethyst, jacinth, agate, crystal, beryl, lapis lazuli, and jasper.

The Twelve Steps of Recovery

- We are powerless and our lives have become unmanageable.
- A power greater than ourselves can restore us to sanity.
- We have decided to turn our will and our lives over to the care of God.
- Take moral inventory of ourselves.
- Admit to God, to ourselves and to others the exact nature of our wrongs.
- We are ready to have God remove all these defects of character.
- We ask God to remove our flaws.
- We make a list of those we have harmed and become willing to make amends to them all.
- We make direct amends to such people wherever possible, except when to do so would injure them or others.
- Continue to take personal inventory and promptly admit when we are wrong.
- Through prayer and meditation, seek to improve our contact with God.
- Carry this message to addicts and practice these principles in all our affairs.

"Examine me O Lord and try me; test my mind and my heart." Psalm 26:2

Are you ready to commit to BEing your BEst self? If yes, how are you going to make the time to read, reflect, and record? What obstacles are standing in your way?

_____

_____

_____

12...52...365...7...24...1,440...

months in a year...weeks in a year...days in a year... days in a week...hours in a day...minutes in a day.

How do you spend your time? How will you spend your time as you BEcome your BEst self?

_____

_____

_____

"And we know that in all things God works for the good of those who love him, who have been called according to his purpose." Romans 8:28

Romans, Chapter 8:28 has reminded me through good and bad days that God calls us for His purpose and His timing is perfect, even when we doubt it. As a control enthusiast, I often behave like Sarah in the Old Testament. Please read Genesis 6 and reflect on her trial. Abraham's wife, Sarah, wanted a baby desperately. She prayed to God continually for a child. When she couldn't wait any longer, she took matters into her own hands. She arranged for her husband and Hagar, a handmaiden, to have a child. He was named Ishmael. Her plan didn't go so well and Ishmael did some pretty awful things. Then, finally at ninety years of age, Sarah became pregnant and named her son Isaac, who became one of the three patriarchs of the Israelites. How many Ishmael's have you had waiting for Isaac?

The questions in this book are designed to open your eyes to the beautiful woman God created you to BE. He knows your purpose. God knows your BEst self and will be BEside you on this journey. Here are some thoughts to get us going:

Describe what you have wanted to BE at various ages. At 10, 20, 30, 40, 50, 60, today?

_____

_____

_____

What do you want to BE today? What changes will make to BEcome your BEst?

_____

_____

_____

How do you BElieve this book will help you BEcome who and what you want to BE?

_____

_____

_____

What do you want to learn about yourself in the next twelve months? What are the strengths you want to capitalize on and the weaknesses you want to manage?

_____

_____

_____

_____

_____

How to Get Your BE 12 Energy to Use This Book!

This is not any book, this is your manual, your journal, a tool in your toolbelt. This book is designed for you to reflect, renew and realize your potential. In my personal experiences and in talking to many of you, I found we were losing our selves to the busyness we call life. Knowing and living our personal values provides the power to BE our BEst. It requires BEing still and committed. Each month you will find an umbrella value and weekly are additional values that require your action. You will find quotes, scriptures, stories and plenty of room to write answers to the provoking questions and action items. Daily, I urge you to write down your prayers in the blanks provided. You will be amazed at what God has answered when you look back at your prayers.

BE AUTHENTIC

CUE THE CURTAIN

BE Authentic

THE FAMOUS AMERICAN FAIRYTALE, *The Wonderful Wizard of Oz,* written by L. Frank Baum, chronicles Dorothy to the magical Land of Oz. The symbolism throughout the book is as meaningful today as it was in 1900 when it was first published. The connection to BEing is not only how Dorothy and new found friends discover they have all they need, but also learn "who" is behind the curtain. The Scarecrow wants a brain, the Tin Man a heart, and the Cowardly Lion wants courage. Those are the three values we need to BE our BEst selves: our mind, our heart, and courage.

Dorothy and her friends endure hardships to find the powerful Oz. Only when the curtain is pulled do they see he is just a man with no special powers. The curtain will be pulled, so BE authentic and live a life illustrative of *your* values.

A favorite children's story, *The Velveteen Rabbit*, by Margery Williams, describes a stuffed rabbit's desire to BE real. He describes that it takes a long time to BEcome and it's not for people who break easy or have sharp edges. It's not beauty that matters and comparing yourself to others is painful. Each time I read this book to our daughters, my eyes welled up because I knew, if I wanted to BE the BEst mom to them, I needed to figure out how to BE the BEst me.

The Velveteen Rabbit promotes values of love, empathy, and compassion and urges us to struggle against what is material and fake. I say with painful honesty that is has taken me fifty years to figure out the importance of authenticity to a joyful, purpose-driven life.

Authenticity is about presence, living in the moment with conviction and confidence, and staying true to yourself. BEing comfortable in your own skin is a process that requires BElieving to thine own self BE true. What that looks like is bringing your '**A** self" to every situation.

Throughout my early career, I didn't talk about myself, my family, and my values in the workplace. I was of the mindset to keep my head down and do my work. In my mid-thirties, with help from mentors and faithful friends, I realized in order to have strong relationships, I needed to bring all my **A**'s to the game. The **A**, or Authentic Amy, needed to show up at home, at work, and at play. Putting my personality and my values together put me on the road to BEing my BEst.

In today's immediate gratification, fast paced, social media consumed world, where it's easy to compare ourselves to others, it is a challenge to be authentic. Instead of seeking to be "fixed", let us consider the one God created and seek to BE our BEst.

BE honest, grateful, and open-minded.

Week 1:

BE Honest

"Above all else, guard your heart, for everything you do flows from it." Proverbs 4:23

I REGRET MY LIES AND THE TIMES I HAVE NOT been honest with myself and others. There it is! It is out there and I am embarrassed. Honesty is about BEing sincere, BEing free from deceit or untruthfulness with yourself and others. If you want a life of joy, do not lie. My father always said, "those who tell white lies are color blind." They miss the brilliance of color as they convince themselves the perceived "good" of the lie is justified. Yet, God is clear about lying. Leviticus 19:11 is clear and simple: "do not lie." And if you need more, read Proverbs 12:22 that reminds us the Lord detests lying lips and delights in truthfulness. Picture God smiling when you choose truth.

There are no small lies to yourself or others. Lying ruins your reputation, leads to a life of deception, and will undermine your relationships. The weight of carrying lies is like running a marathon with a cement block on your back. One lie becomes two, becomes three, four, and beyond. Dishonest people lose the ability to tell the difference between truth and lies. If you think you have anxiety, tell a few lies, and watch the chaos multiply. You will alienate yourself from people. Here's the truth: do not fool your-self, people know a liar. Do you want to be trusted? Tell the truth.

I found the value of honesty in a dark valley. Early in my lobbying career, I was the managing partner of a national lobbying firm, I had the privilege to represent a variety of nationally recognized clients. With the support of my part-ners, we were thoughtful in taking clients whose causes we valued and in declining those whose causes alerted our "gut radar." One of the valuable causes was leading a regional growth management process. I worked with brilliant people from across the country collaborating on convening a critical dialogue about the community I called home. The project was personal because this region was where I chose to move, raise my children, and start a business. The work was hard, and the hours were long, yet incredibly rewarding. We reached out to over 10,000 people and convened over 300 leaders to focus on transportation, housing, business, and healthcare. We accomplished much.

During this time, our firm worked with a client who was thoughtfully and deliberately developing a part of the region into a thriving live/work/play community. Yet, no good deed goes undone. A local female reporter decided she had a different story and selectively gathered her facts. The story she wanted to tell about me was that I was con-flicted and trying to destroy the community I called home.

Sister, there are insecure women who will work to ruin you. No matter how many times you speak the truth, some will still lie about you. Lowering to their level is no BEnefit to your growth. BE the change you want to see in others. The details are irrelevant today. Yet I share this painful story to remind you that it is takes grit to live your values. There will be those that stand with you and for you. And there will be those that will try to destroy you. BE honest with yourself and never compromise.

To make this season more challenging, I was regularly traveling from Florida to Kentucky to help care for my father who was recently diagnosed with Pick's Disease, a rare form of dementia. On a trip back, the reporter called with a few questions. It was obvious she did not care about the answers or truth. She shared that I would be the feature of an editorial the next morning. I was numb and sick. I prayed and asked God for wisdom and peace. The fear was overwhelming as I worried that the strong reputation I had worked diligently to achieve would be ruined by lies. I reached out to my village for wisdom. My wise partners and brilliant mentors, Paul, Chris, and David, resonated the same theme: "Can you sleep at night?" The answer was yes. I knew I was honest and I gave her all the facts. At four in the morning, I read the editorial. It is in your darkest moments that you dig for your own strengths and you know your real friends. My faith became stronger each day. God led me out of the pit and I faced my lions. I survived and vowed that no one would tell my story.

My values were tested and it was hard to forgive. We are God's creation and we all sin. We are inherently good and inherently bad and we are full of mistakes. The bitterness against this woman continued for longer than I care to admit. She later lost her job and I lost track of her. Six months later, a burning bush set my heart ablaze. One of my mentors and lifeboats, Father John Hiers, delivered a sermon on forgiveness. When you forgive, you free the prisoner, and the prisoner is you. God's Word reminds us to forgive. John referenced the following:

- *"And be kind to one another, tenderhearted, forgiving one another, just as God in Christ also forgave you."* *Ephesians 4:32*
- When Peter asked how many times he should forgive those who sinned against him, *"Jesus answered,' I tell you, not just seven times, but seventy times seven!'"* *Matthew 18:22*
- *"For if you forgive men for their transgressions, your Heavenly Father will also forgive you; but if you do not forgive men, then your Father will not forgive your transgressions."* Matthew 6:14-15

This book is not about forgiveness, but I can tell you, I am happier today because of God's grace and love, and because I have forgiven people that have hurt me. I hope you will do the same. Seek wise counsel if you are trying to forgive someone or yourself. Archbishop Desmund Tutu in *The Book of Forgiving* reminds us that forgiveness does not relieve someone of responsibility or erase accountability. When you forgive, you are freeing yourself, not turning a blind eye.

DAY 1

"Do not lie to each other since you have taken off your old self with its practices." Colossians 3:9

MY "OLD SELF" WASN'T MY BEST SELF. JUST LIKE taking off sweaty clothes or dirty socks, rid yourself of the cinder block that is keeping you from your BEst self.

Steps four and five of the Twelve Steps to Recovery call us to search our moral inventory and amend any wrong we have committed.

As you reflect on your inventory, how is your honesty? Has your dishonesty created a wrong that needs amending? Do you seek forgiveness? Have you said I am sorry and meant it? What is God calling you to do today?

_____

_____

_____

_____

_____

_____

_____

_____

_____

Prayer:

_____

Day 2

"No temptation has overtaken you except what is common to mankind. And God is faithful; he will not let you be tempted beyond what you can bear. But when you are tempted, he will provide a way out." 1 Corinthians 10:13

THIS IS GOING TO HURT, SO GET THE BAND-aids. Describe and dissect a lie you are living with today. Maybe you are lying to yourself right now about an addiction or unhealthy decisions you are making. God will always provide a way out. Do you need to make amends with someone? If yes, do it today. Now *forgive* yourself, because God forgives you.

_____

_____

_____

_____

_____

_____

_____

_____

Prayer:

_____

Day 3

"The man of integrity walks securely, but he who takes crooked paths will be found out." Proverbs 10:9

YOU CAN'T BE HONEST WITH OTHERS IF YOU are not first honest with yourself. What paths are you on where you are fooling yourself? Describe a time that your lies were revealed and how you corrected the path.

_____

_____

_____

_____

_____

_____

_____

_____

_____

_____

_____

_____

Prayer:

_____

Day 4

"For we are taking pains to do what is right, not only in the eyes of the Lord but also in the eyes of man." 2 Corinthians 8:21

CHANGE THE THINGS THAT MAKE YOU LIE. ARE you in a job or relationship that forces you to lie to make yourself look better? Are you surrounded with friends that tell you there's broccoli in your teeth or "friends" that don't bring out the best in you? What changes do you need to make to reveal your authentic self?

_____

_____

_____

_____

_____

_____

_____

_____

_____

_____

_____

Prayer:

_____

Day 5

"Do unto others as you would have them do unto you." Luke 6:31

GOSSIPING IS A FORM OF DISHONESTY. IT IS deceitful and never ends well. Fight the urge to talk about someone. If you are in a conversation, and you see the gossip train barreling down the track, purposely pause. Stop what you are about to say and think of when you have been the victim of lying tongues. BEcome a BEacon of truth by redirecting the conversation to a new topic. Describe a situation when you gossiped about someone and how you felt after you reflected on the conversation.

_____

_____

_____

_____

_____

_____

_____

_____

_____

Prayer:

_____

Week 2:

BE Grateful

"I will give thanks to you, Lord, with all my heart; I will tell of all your wonderful deeds. I will be glad and rejoice in you." Psalm 9:1-2

I AM BLESSED BEYOND MEASURE. LET ME TELL you about my BEloved husband and daughters and you will see how they fill my grateful bucket. Twenty-five years ago, this handsome, athletic, brilliant man came into my life. Sean is my soul mate and while I could fill a book with our love story, his strengths have given me a life of love and happiness. Sean always put me and our daughters above other priorities. He is compassionate and patient and his solid approach keeps me grounded. Megan and Molly are simply gifts from God. Above their beauty—inside and out—wit and athleticism, focus and passion, they are kind and loving. While I am not claiming anything is perfect about my family or my life, I am proclaiming they bring out the BEst in me, on most days.

The word "gratitude" is derived from the Latin word, *gratia,* meaning grace. *Whoa!* Pause and think about how God's grace is given to you. Grace is God's blessing to us even though we don't deserve it.

God gave me another chance at life after my "spell." He saved my daughter and mother from peril in their car wreck.

He is healing many people I love. He has given me many second chances. God is great!

We choose happiness. Research and the realm of psychology strongly corelates gratitude to happiness. Grateful people have long term happiness and more fulfilling relationships. They are more content and less materialistic, more empathetic and forgiving with lower levels of stress, and sleep more deeply. Grateful people display their spirituality. I choose to be grateful and happy!

Cultivating a grateful spirit requires energy. BEing grateful is a deliberate recognition of the blessings surrounding us. It reminds us we are not in control. God provides endless treasures waiting to be recognized. A grateful heart is so full that there is no room for complaining. BE purposeful in your gratefulness and make it visible. Keep a grateful basket for you and your family, create a journal and record your grateful gifts.

What could have been a tragic event on February 23 became one of the my most grateful. Earlier, I mentioned the call I received that my mother, Rosemary, and Molly, my fourteen-year-old daughter, were in a car accident. I was about twenty miles away and as I frantically rushed across a bridge, I begged God that they were safe. I always ask myself why the best conversations with God are when we are at our worst. Looking across Tampa Bay, I felt God's hand on my shoulder and heard Him whisper, "Trust me."

I kept praying and when I arrived at the trauma center, I was shocked to find my daughter, Molly, speaking with a police officer recounting the story. This chick is gritty with a "get it done" attitude. It wasn't until I went to see the car and the damage to the passenger side where Molly was riding, that I fell to my knees. I will never understand God's love and grace that she walked away from that accident.

Rosemary, on the other hand, was pretty banged up with multiple injuries. One of the biggest blessings of this accident was she moved in with our family. I am grateful for the opportunity to care for her and the lessons God taught us as she healed. My mom and I spent months together and between doctor's visits, cooking, and some fast food runs, we reconnected.

DAY 1

"Cultivate the habit of being grateful for every good
thing that comes to you and give thanks continuously."
Ralph Waldo Emerson

BEGIN YOUR GRATITUDE JOURNAL. FIND A
journal small enough that you can keep in your purse or
somewhere close to you. Or if you have a planner or note-
cards, make them available for easy reference. Begin your
attitude of gratitude by writing down five blessings.

_____

_____

_____

_____

_____

_____

_____

_____

_____

_____

_____

_____

Prayer:

_____

Day 2

"Give thanks in all circumstances; for this is the will of God in Christ Jesus for you." 1 Thessalonians 5:18

THE UNDENIABLE POWER OF GRATITUDE ARTICLE in Huffpost reminds us that gratitude brings greater meaning to our lives. Gratitude is a decision and my gratitude journal has carried me through the most difficult times in my life. Describe a difficult time in your life. Was it a job change? A move? A divorce? Recall the situation and write about how you coped. Did you cling to friends and counselors or was pounding a stiff drink every day your remedy? By making the attitude of gratitude my way of life, I have found the rainbows in the rain and the stars in the dark. Describe how gratitude has helped you thrive in a difficult time.

_____

_____

_____

In addition to your prayer today, continue your *attitude of gratitude* daily as you record at least one grateful gift.

_____

_____

_____

Prayer:

_____

Day 3

"Therefore, let us be grateful for receiving a kingdom that cannot be shaken, and thus let us offer to God acceptable worship, with reverence and awe." Hebrews 12:28

GRATEFUL PEOPLE VALUE GIFTS OF ALL SIZES and shapes. What grateful gifts surround you? An awesome sunset, a beautiful tree in your neighborhood? Pause and look around and describe the beauty God has put in front of you.

_____

_____

_____

_____

_____

_____

_____

_____

_____

Prayer:

_____

Grateful Gift:

_____

Day 4

"I do not cease to give thanks for you, remembering you in my prayers." Ephesians 1:16

WRITE SOME THANK YOU NOTES. PREFERABLY, handwrite and mail notes of appreciation to a friend, family member, teacher, the song leader at church, your child or spouse, or a coworker. For more motivation visit spreadthanks.com. Your thoughtfulness will brighten their day and yours. If you don't want to buy the stamp, an email might suffice. When was the last time you received a thank you note? When was the last time you wrote one? How did these occasions make you feel? List some people that need a thank you from you. Mark your calendar to thank someone once a week.

_____

_____

_____

_____

_____

_____

_____

_____

_____

Prayer:

_____

Grateful Gift:

_____

Day 5

"Thanks be to God for his inexpressible gift." 2 Corinthians 9:15

LINDSAY HOLMES IN HER ARTICLE, *10 THINGS Grateful People Do Different,* describes that living a good life includes counting our blessings. These ten habits will help you cultivate an *attitude of gratitude*.

1. Journal.
2. Don't avoid the negative.
3. Spend time with loved ones, and.
4. Tell them you love them.
5. Use social media *mindfully*.
6. Know the value of the little things, and.
7. Help others appreciate them too.
8. Volunteer.
9. Exercise.
10. Love themselves.

Which of these do you do? Explain how and talk about which ones from this list you plan to do better.

_____

_____

_____

_____

_____

_____

Prayer:

_____

Grateful Gift:

_____

Week 3

BE Open Minded

"So, God created mankind in his own image, in the image of God he created them, male and female, he created them." Genesis 1:27

AUTHENTIC PEOPLE KNOW WHO THEY ARE AND that for what they stand. They live their values. With media bombarding us from every angle, discerning hearts and minds are required. We read editorials, we hear neighbors, friends, politicians, and business leaders spouting facts, opinions, and often in disrespectful tones with cruel words. Some people surround themselves with like-minded thinkers. Others desire to grow by seeking different opinions from diverse groups of people.

To BE open-minded, remove your personal bias and pre-judgments to see that God created everyone for a purpose.

You value diversity when your mind is open to see and understand the differences of others. My daughters teach me how to BE my BEst open-minded self. Teens today have a closer view of diversity of sexual preference, education, religion, color, and creed than my generation.

One afternoon, I was sharing with Molly a conversation I had with another parent. To be honest, I find this parent pompous. He always talks about his child, compares them, and exaggerates their talents. I made a not-so-kind comment about him one day when I had reached my breaking point. Molly caught me and called me "judgy." Yikes, arrow to the heart. And she was right. I was not BEing open minded, respectful, and was not honoring someone different from me.

To BE open-minded, we must commit to accept and respect others who are not like us. There is diversity in race, religion, learning, culture, and so on. BEgin to recognize the differences around you. BE bold and do not tolerate others who poke fun and use cruel words to those of a different variety.

Looking in my mirror has given me the reality of my differences. While not formally tested, I am likely dyslexic. Dyslexia hasn't stopped me from running several companies, writing legislation, obtaining a BS, BA, and MBA, reading and speaking French, reading at least one book a month, and writing a book. Gal pals, realizing my differences, opened my mind and heart to understanding the value of differences. Understanding how I am unique, and learning facts about my traits, opened my eyes. I learned as much about Dyslexia as I could, and I learned skills to maximize my abilities. The American Dyslexia Association is a great source for facts about this condition. Their website provides the following:

- It is estimated that one in ten people have dyslexia and they don't all mix up letters or have difficulty reading.

- Over forty million American adults are dyslexic and only two million know it.
- Dyslexia is not tied to IQ. Einstein was dyslexic and had an estimated IQ of 160.
- Dyslexia has nothing to do with not working hard.
- Over fifty percent of NASA employees are dyslexic.
- There are varieties of learning styles and not every dyslexic is the same. Know the facts.

Our tool belt is full of tools to help recognize and celebrate diversity. Hammer that home.

Day 1

"Draw near to God, and he will draw near to you." James 1:8

DESCRIBE HOW YOU ARE DIFFERENT FROM others. Don't hold back—this is your chance to talk about your uniqueness.

Prayer:

Grateful Gift:

Day 2

"Stop judging by appearances, but instead judge correctly." John 7:24

To be open-minded, let go of some control. As a "control enthusiast", this is incredibly hard for me. What challenge are you dealing with at work, or with a family member or a friend that needs you to see from their point of view?

When we change our minds, we can change anything.

What questions do you need to ask? How can you see their point of view today? How can you BE open-minded by seeing another's point of view?

_____

_____

_____

_____

_____

_____

_____

_____

Prayer:

_____

Grateful Gift:

_____

DAY 3

"Finally, brothers and sisters, whatever is true, whatever is noble, whatever is right, whatever is pure, whatever lovely, whatever is admirable – if anything is excellent or praiseworthy – think about such things."
Philippians 4:8

DESCRIBE HOW YOU SPENT TODAY THINKING on what is true, lovely, and admirable in those around you.

I spent thirty days trying to live this Scripture. My tricks were to write down the words and describe how I displayed each adjective. It changed my attitude of judging others and opened my mind and heart to the beauty of others. Beside each word below describe how you think and live these values. When someone is trying your patience or you are having a bad day it may be easier to be negative, what actions can you make to 'think about these things?'

True _____

_____

_____

Noble _____

_____

_____

Right _____

_____

_____

Pure _____

_____

_____

Admirable _____

_____

_____

Praiseworthy_____

_____

_____

Prayer:

_____

Grateful Gift:

_____

Day 4

*"There is neither Jew nor Greek, there is neither slave
nor free, there is no male and female, for you are all
one in Christ Jesus." Galatians 3:28*

DESCRIBE AREAS THAT CHALLENGE YOU TO SEE
that we are all created equal. Are there specific areas of your
life where you need to be open to new ideas? Do you need
to try new foods, go to new places, meet someone new, read
a newspaper that has opinions different from yours? Do
you need to learn about a new culture, talk to someone in
your neighborhood, friend circle, or co-worker that doesn't
look or think like you? Reflect on how these interactions
opened your mind.

_____

_____

_____

_____

_____

_____

_____

Prayer:

_____

Grateful Gift:

_____

Day 5

"As for me and my household, we will serve the Lord."
Joshua 29:15

OPEN YOUR MIND LIKE A PARACHUTE AND LET information work for you. Be unprejudiced in situations you encounter today. At the grocery store, the office, at home, and with friends and family. Fight the urge to react when you hear or see something that is different. Put yourself in another's shoes today and reflect on how you have grown. There are angels everywhere of every color and personality. As you observe your surroundings today, share the times that you caught yourself in judgment because of appearance. What does judging righteously mean to you?

_____

_____

_____

_____

_____

_____

_____

Prayer:

_____

Grateful Gift:

_____

REVEAL your REAL

"You were taught, with regard to your former way of life, to put off your old self, which is being corrupted by its deceitful desires; to be made new in the attitude of your minds; and to put on the new self, created to be like God in true righteousness and holiness." Ephesians 4:22-24

Day 1

Describe how this first month has opened your eyes to yourself and your value system. Do you break easily, do you have sharp edges, and what does BEing *Real* mean to you? What obstacles, fear, or someone else's agenda can you identify that might stop you from revealing your real?

_____

_____

Day 2

"You will keep in peace those whose minds are steadfast because they trust in you." Isaiah 26:3

Carol Dweck is a leading expert on mindset. In her best-selling book, *Mindset, the New Psychology of Success,* she describes growth and fixed mindsets. The growth mindset believes strengths are cultivated through your efforts, strategies, and help from others. In the fixed mindset, people believe their basic qualities, like their intelligence or talent, are simply fixed traits. When you have a growth mindset, you believe you are in control of your own abilities and that dedication and hard work will lead to the success you seek.

Are you willing to live this year in the growth mindset? In other words, do you BElieve you can maximize your strengths and develop your best qualities through strategies, work, and commitment? *And*, can you seek help from others? If yes, what traits do you have that reflect the growth mindset?

_____

_____

Day 3

"To see thee more clearly, love thee more dearly, and follow thee more nearly."

You may have heard this in music, from the, pulpit or in a Bible study. This phrase was a part of a 40 day fast that my gal pal Jules and I completed during some challenging work times. Realizing the power of a "chant" of sorts, I select a focus word every January 1. Joy, impact, faith, trust, and focus have been some of the words that have helped me BE on purpose over the years.

Do you have a mantra that you repeat regularly? What is it? Why does it motivate you? If you do not, find one today that motivates you. It can be a quote, Scripture, or wisdom you have learned from others.

_____

_____

Day 4

Who is the most *real* person you know? What makes this person authentic? What qualities do they possess that you need? If you need to spend time learning from them, reach out and visit.

_____

_____

Day 5

What does your value system look like today? What activity or piece of information most challenged you during the past few weeks?

_____

_____

BE CONFIDENT

To Walk on Water, Get Out of the Boat.

Be Confident

Lift up your heads. Psalm 24;9a

As a mother of two amazing teenaged girls, I am obsessed with self-esteem. Our daughters, Megan and Molly, continue to accomplish their goals because they believe in themselves. Some of my favorite memories as Megan and Molly were growing up, were their numerous friends hanging out in our home. I learned so much from them, their parents who lingered at our home and the giggles of babies growing into ladies. No matter your age, find gal pals that build your confidence and bring out your BEst.

One of the most valuable lessons I learned about my role as a mother of girls was from our first pediatrician. When we took our now seventeen-year-old daughter to her one-month checkup appointment, we were presented with the physician of a lifetime. Dr. Jean Bennett became our first pediatrician. This is not just any woman or any doctor. Dr. Bennett was the *first* female graduate of University of Florida's College of Medicine. She was a member of the college's charter class of 1960. She practiced for more than forty years in Clearwater, was the president of the medical staff at a local hospital and named Florida Pediatrician of the Year in 1984. Bennett took her children on house calls, hired a trusting caretaker to help, ate breakfast and dinner as a family and carved out time for church. Despite reading all I could about what to expect at the first doctor's appointment, I was nervous and had many questions. Will these vaccines have an adverse impact on my child? Are there side effects? Will she cry? Dr. Bennett walked in like an angel full of joy and life. She went through the exam, explained in detail all she was doing and at the end, she said, "Sit down, let's talk." I recall her heartfelt wisdom like it was yesterday. Her words, *"Teach her self-esteem!"* still resonate today. Girls with positive self-esteem are less likely to get pregnant, be mixed up with the wrong crowd, and more likely to become productive, focused citizens. I left that office that day with a beautiful one month old and a mission to teach our daughter positive self-esteem. Not only is our first daughter full of self-esteem, she is a brilliant, loving young lady about to embark on her next chapter. Praise to God for blessing us with Dr. Bennett.

Let us BE real about women with confidence and those without. Think of some women you know that exude confidence. They believe in themselves and they do not waste their valuable time striking down others with words and actions. They spend their time lifting up others. Life coach, Kali Rogers describes the qualities of confident women. Confident women:

- Admit their flaws
- Say no
- Listen

- Don't conform
- Are open to love
- Ask for help
- Own their feelings
- Release guilt
- Support others

I believe confident women present themselves physically also. They walk into a room with presence. They begin a conversation having thought it through thoroughly. They stand up straight and look people in the eye. While many critics comment on women's attire, their makeup or hair, the truth is, do what feels good to you. I have found when I feel like I look good, I am good.

My first mentor was a Fifth Third Bank female executive named Carolyn McCoy. We met every month during my banking career and she provided me great wisdom that has carried me through the last thirty years. She said, "Hold up your head, walk with purpose, and. . . always smile."

There is scientific proof that good posture is vital for confidence. Rule number one in Jordan Peterson's bestselling book, *12 Rules for Life,* is "Stand up straight with your shoulders back." The book is a good read and not just because he too understands the value of twelve. In this rule, he describes the anatomy of a lobster and how serotonin and octopamine are critical in defeat and victory. For your biology reference, serotonin is the happy chemical that contributes to your well-being, good mood, appetite, sleep, and memory. Octopamine is a neurotransmitter found in invertebrates. A lobster with high levels of serotonin and low levels of octopamine is a cocky, strutting shellfish, much less likely to back down when challenged. The lobster with high serotonin and low octopamine is the victor. The opposite neurochemical configuration, a high ratio of octopamine to serotonin, produces a defeated-looking, scrunched-up, inhibited, drooping sort of lobster likely to disappear at the first hint of trouble. Stand up straight!

Great accomplishments occur when women bind together. When we stop judging other women for their figure, skills, clothes, perfect children and career, we can start tackling what's important. Empower yourself to be confident and not worry about them, but instead look how your skills complement theirs. The BEst accessory we can own is confidence.

BE courageous, well spoken, well read, and women wi\$e.

WEEK 1

BE Courageous

"Be strong and of good courage, do not fear nor be afraid of them for the Lord your God will be with you wherever you go. He will never leave you nor forsake you." Deuteronomy 31:6

IN THE BIBLE, "COURAGE" IS REFERRED TO AS good cheer. Fear and I don't get along. It's an emotion I don't handle well and it wasn't until my fiftieth year of turmoil and heartache that I learned how to say to fear, "Not today." To understand my battle with fear is to know I am risk taker, pull up your boot straps and storm the castle gal. Parenting teenage girls, and maybe boys, is a confidence killer. Fear manages to sneak right in and tries to own you when you are at your weakest. A favorite song lifted me when fear was trying to tell my story. *The Breakup Song* by Francesca Battistelli is a must for your play list. Here are few phrases as you turn up the volume loud. "I know who I am. I know I'm strong...So fear, you will never be welcome here." My biggest fear during my daughter's senior year was that I missed teaching her some valuable lesson. And that, ladies, is why finishing this book during my fiftieth year became of critical importance.

Fear is mentioned 365 times in the Bible. God encourages us to trust Him and not to be afraid, every day. He

43

urges us to let *go*. Psalm 23 reminds us that even though we walk through the darkest valley, we should not be afraid. God will protect and comfort us. The journaling this week helped me build rituals of kicking fear to the curb.

We fear failure. We are afraid we aren't a good enough mother, daughter, boss, wife, cook, decorator. . . the list continues. We cannot overcome our fear of failure until we accept that we are not perfect, but we *are perfect* in God's eyes. He has created us to be exactly who we are today.

My failure list is pretty long and the lessons I learned from each of those is longer. Failure has given me the first-hand experience to wrestle with what I did and build a BEtter self. Each failure made me a bit more resilient and a lot more focused on achieving my BEst.

DAY 1

"Take courage! It is I. Do not be afraid." Matthew 14:27

THE STORY OF JESUS WALKING ON WATER IS one of my favorites. Matthew 14:22 begins with Jesus walking to a mountainside alone to pray. His disciples go ahead on a boat. As evening falls, wind and waves begin. Jesus walks on the water from the shore and His disciples fear "it's a ghost." Jesus says, "Take courage."

Today, hold courage in your head and your heart, for these organs are the ones that keep you alive.

Being brave is an attitude. A few years ago, I made a difficult career decision. I let myself get in the way and left an amazing organization for what I thought was a step forward. In reflection, I know God's hand was on the move. Instead of trusting my God, I tried to do it alone. That "step forward" I coin now as my "lost year." That year, I lost myself, my pride, and "friends." Yet, I found a deeper walk on the water with God. He held my hand through the crashing waves and took me safely to the shore.

Please read Matthew 14:22-35. Do you feel like Peter and ask, "Lord, save me"? Do you need to BE courageous with a decision or another area of your life today? Write about it. Or if you have recently been brave with an issue, describe the situation. What did you learn and is the outcome what you expected? How did you trust God to help you get out of the boat?

_____

_____

_____

_____

_____

_____

_____

_____

_____

_____

_____

_____

_____

_____

_____

_____

_____

_____

_____

Prayer:

_____

Grateful Gift:

_____

Day 2

"Being confident of this, that he who began a good work in you will carry it on to completion until the day of Christ Jesus." Philippians 1:6

THE OLD TESTAMENT TELLS THE STORY OF Benaiah, a David loyalist, who goes into a pit on snowy day and kills a lion. His story reminds us that our biggest regrets may be the lions we were too afraid to chase. Read 2 Samuel 23:20. All we know of Benaiah is that he is a valiant warrior who performed great exploits. His bravery and loyalty lead him to the high honor in King Solomon's army.

Is there a lion staring you in the face? Write about a time you were brave. Was it a crucial conversation you needed to have with a friend or loved one? Was it a career change? BE descriptive and focused on the situation and circumstances and describe your courage to chase the lion. What happened and what did you learn? What was the hardest step in this situation?

_____

_____

_____

Prayer:

_____

Grateful Gift:

_____

Day 3

"I come against you in the name of the Lord."
1 Samuel 17:45

THE STORY OF DAVID AND GOLIATH IS A STORY
of courage, faith, and overcoming what feels impossible. The
message is relevant in many walks of life. Read 1 Samuel,
Chapter 17 and learn more about David and his courage.

Describe David and how are you similar and different
from him in this story.

_____

_____

Who is your Goliath? What sling and stone from God's
Word and values can you use to fight this giant?

_____

_____

_____

_____

_____

_____

Prayer:

_____

Grateful Gift:

_____

Day 4

"For the spirit God gave us does not make us timid, but gives us power, love and self-discipline." 2 Timothy 1:7

COURAGE REQUIRES CONFIDENCE. YOU ARE good at many things. Make lists of your amazing talents, skills, and attributes. *Really!* Don't say, "I'll do this later." Set the clock for ten minutes and write them down.

_____

_____

_____

_____

_____

_____

_____

_____

_____

_____

Prayer:

_____

Grateful Gift:

_____

Day 5

"If any of you lacks wisdom, you should ask God, who gives generously to all without finding fault, and it will be given to you." James 1:5

WHAT DECISION (S) ARE YOU FACING THAT require courage? What tools do you need to tackle this decision. Every day, I pray this for myself, Sean, Megan, and Molly:

Gracious God provide us discerning hearts to know right from wrong and a critical thinking mind that seeks your wisdom.

_____

_____

_____

_____

_____

_____

_____

_____

Prayer:

_____

Grateful Gift:

_____

WEEK 2

BE WELL SPOKEN
AND WELL READ

"The more that you read, the more things you will
know. The more you learn, the more places you'll go."
Dr. Seuss

THE VALUES WE ARE DISCUSSING THIS WEEK ARE vulnerable spots for me. Sister, you are probably a great communicator, and I know I shouldn't compare myself to you, but I am jealous of you for that skill. I am a simple girl from Kentucky, and I regret to say I did not read enough to build a strong vocabulary. And not identifying the skills I could have implored due to my learning style, Dyslexia, didn't help.

Well, it came to full light when I started my first job. After college, I landed a job at Fifth Third Bank in the management training program in Cincinnati, Ohio. The program provided rotations in various departments. My first was Human Resources and the vice president, Dan, was a tough man. I worked directly with him and one day sent him a memo regarding one of my projects. Oh my! The next thing I knew, this man was screaming about tense, verb use, typos. He stood over me with more red on my memo than a trauma scene. Luckily, my direct manager immersed me in a vocabulary course. To her, I am eternally grateful.

For the last thirty years I have fought to improve my skills by reading, deliberate proofreading, read at least one book a month, utilize the daily word of the day, attend seminars, and seek input from others. Today, my vocabulary is strong as I pay attention to my words and usage.

Strong communicators not only know what to say but when to say it. Too often, I say something to someone I care about before thinking it through. Armed with the wisdom from my executive coach, Kathleen, I follow this approach to important conversations

- BE prepared. Write down what you need to say, rehearse, and seek to understand the person or group to whom you will be speaking.
- BE well read. Do your research and gather the facts.
- BE well spoken. Your words matter. Choose them carefully and consider how they will be interpreted.
- THINK. Are your words True, Helpful, Inspiring, Necessary, and Kind?

Be well read. It is proven through volumes of research that reading is critical for communication and continual brain development. Don't just fit in, stand out. The benefits of reading include:

- Builds imagination
- Increases focus and concentration
- Improves memory
- Helps with communication

Day 1

"May the words of my mouth and this meditation of my heart be pleasing in your sight, Lord, my Rock and my Redeemer." Psalm 19:14

I WISH ALL MY CONVERSATIONS WERE PLEASING in God's sight. I have had a lot of crucial conversations over the last twelve months. Recently, I needed to share my failure with a friend and wanted her forgiveness. I wrote five different scripts so that when I became emotional, I would have the points I needed to communicate.

What conversations are you having today that require your preparation? Write your key points, the why, what, and the words you will use.

_____

_____

_____

_____

_____

_____

_____

Prayer:

_____

Grateful Gift:

_____

Day 2

"Do not let any unwholesome talk come out of your mouths, but only what is helpful for encouraging others according to their needs, that it may benefit those who listen." Ephesians 4:29

I DO NOT LIKE TO HEAR PROFANITY. I BELIEVE women are above it and can communicate without using corrupt talk. I don't know the purpose it serves and while I can yell a good curse word, I regret it as soon as it rolls off my lips.

The same is true of profane words against people. Words can lift up or tear down. You may not realize this, but your words and actions are being watched from every direction.

What words will you choose today? Will they be encouraging to others? Think about your words today and ask if it is unwholesome, unbecoming or just mean. Maybe try to genuinely compliment at least three people today. Make it genuine. Plenty of people are worthy of your praise.

_____

_____

_____

_____

Prayer:

_____

Grateful Gift:

_____

Day 3

"The tongue also is a fire, a world of evil among the parts of the body. It corrupts the whole body, sets the whole course of one's life on fire, and is itself set on fire by hell." James 3:6

READ JAMES 3:3-6. ARE YOU CHALLENGED LIKE me in that holding your tongue can be like steering the Titanic? And many words from my tongue are like the iceberg that sunk the Titanic. I have learned the hard way that you catch more flies with honey than vinegar and the stinging words may leave a permanent scar.

Describe a time or two that you could have held your tongue in a fiery exchange. What would those conversations have sounded like if you would have paused and considered your words? Now, describe interactions where your words were positive and uplifting.

_____

_____

_____

_____

_____

_____

_____

Prayer:

_____

Grateful Gift:

_____

Day 4

*"With the tongue we praise our Lord and Father, and
with it we curse human beings, who have been made
in God's likeness." James 3:9*

MY GREATEST GAL PALS DO NOT SPEAK NEGA-
tively about other people. For fifteen years, through preg-
nancies, parenting pressures, fishing, and laughter, my
friend Ann and I have probably walked over 1,000 miles
together. There have been circumstances where she could
have spoken negative of others, and she always chose praise
and positive words. Two other gal pals, Tiffany and Katja,
never fill their time with negative talk about others. These
friends have humbled me and reminded me to choose
words well.

Read James 3:9-13. Instead of words that curse others,
how will you praise them? Write down all the positive
words you gave others today or the ones you plan to give.

_____

_____

_____

_____

_____

Prayer:

_____

Grateful Gift:

_____

Day 5

MASTER THE FIVE-PARAGRAPH ESSAY. PICK A topic, be creative, have fun, and write it now. Don't put it off. You need this in your toolbox.

The format of essay should have five paragraphs: one introductory paragraph, three body paragraphs with support and development, and one concluding paragraph.

_____

_____

_____

_____

_____

_____

_____

_____

_____

_____

_____

Prayer:

_____

Grateful Gift:

_____

Week 3

BE Women Wi$e

Buckle up and get ready to change your life! Unlike other chapters in this book, this chapter encompasses a permanent lifestyle change, so the tips here are things you will do not only for this week, but for the rest of your life. Open your mind and heart and start a new to-do list.

This week, you will get started on making permanent changes to the way you view, manage, and spend your money.

This week is not about shame or blame, but about accountability and taking control of your life. This week is about why and how to stop comparing yourself to others and trying to keep up with the Joneses. This week is about understanding that our job titles, bank balances, and debt do not define us.

This week is about BEcoming informed, educated, and engaged.

One of the most undermining fallacies females hear is that girls aren't good at math. I do not know the origin of this useless idea, but I need you to help us all break it because it is breaking us. We are not lazy or stupid, but somewhere along the way, many women begin to think they are not skilled at math, finance, and making and managing their own money. This belief sabotages our ability to be financially independent and successful.

The Global Financial Literacy Excellence Center reported in 2015 that only 12% of US Women could answer three basic questions about financial literacy. We have made great strides in so many areas, including education, employment, and wealth. It is time for you to own your finances and the responsibility to provide for yourself and others.

In 2017, a Forbes article, *Why Have Women's Economic Power Surged? Five Stats you Need to Know*, provided information about the financial role women play in the economy. Today, more than forty percent of women in the US are the primary breadwinners for their families with children under 18. Another twenty-two are co-breadwinners with their spouses. Women also control more than fifty percent of the country's personal wealth. This means women are expected to take charge of $22 trillion of the nation's expected $44 trillion in total personal wealth by 2020. It is vital that we empower ourselves to take control of our financial health and take advantage of every opportunity to make our money work for us.

I am not a financial advisor and would not presume to tell you how to spend, save, or invest your money. What I do know from years of stress and anxiety over money, is that the simple tips in this chapter will help you to *be women wi$e*. If you apply them, you will reap enormous rewards.

The values we have discussed throughout this book should shed light on the ways you spend, save, and invest. Keep your life free from the love of money and be content with what you have, because God has said, *"I will never leave or forsake you" Hebrews 13:5.*

I Did It and You Can Too

I have set many financial goals for myself over the years. I started working when I was fourteen and while my parents did an amazing job of providing for and educating me, I knew my financial future was my responsibility. I stumbled and often found myself in uncomfortable financial situations.

At forty-five, I set a goal to be debt-free at fifty years of age. I knew I had to get serious. It wasn't easy, but here's what I did to reach my goal:

- I stopped getting pedicures and manicures.
- I went on spending hiatus for three to five months and purchased only at consignment shops where I had credit from the items I sold there.
- I made money and budgeting a family project, and we committed as a family to simplifying our lives and spending less money.
- We reduced the number of times we ate out. Instead, I started planning and cooking meals at home and diligently grocery shopping with coupons.
- We limited our travel.

I also sought expert help from many sources. The Penny Hoarder (www.pennyhoarder.com) is one of my favorites. It was created by a brilliant man, Kyle Taylor, who, after finding himself deeply in debt, has dedicated his life to helping others BE financially secure. The site is a resource and inspiration. It contains thousands of meaningful tips for saving and making money and real success stories.

I have also learned a lot from Dave Ramsey and Suze Orman, who are nationally recognized experts in financial sustainability.

If you are serious and ready for painful change resulting in joyful dollars, read any of their books. Some of Dave's tips that I have found useful include:

- Make a budget and spending plan.
- Commit to change.
- Manage your finances.
- Have a specific plan for every dollar to avoid impulse spending.
- Live within your means.
- Be frugal now to build wealth in the future.
- Do everything you can to get out of debt. *Everything!*
- Don't borrow money or use charge cards.
- Save for unexpected expenses.
- Invest in your future.

Instead of daily activities, this week you need to address the tasks in this chapter at your own pace. Resist the urge to put this off. Read through this chapter every day and own the tasks. Put them on your to-do list. Even though you probably won't get around to fully implementing them this week, you should at least get started.

Take Responsibility for Your Financial Stability

Do not depend on someone else to take care of you. Maybe you have rich uncle who you think might leave you money someday. Don't stake your financial future on it. Countless things can happen to prevent you from receiving such a windfall, so plan your budget without factoring in any money that is not fully under your control.

Maybe you already have a family trust or have come into a nice inheritance. If so, that is super news and congratulations! But even if you receive such a gift, no matter how large or small, it is your job to protect it and manage it carefully. Take this from my personal experience: there is no shortage of people who are willing to lie and steal to take your money from you.

That's why it's hugely important to have a strong, inviolable plan for controlling your spending, saving money, and investing it for maximum return on a consistent basis, no matter what money you expect to fall on you in the future.

Remember this: Saving reflects your values. Spending reflects your ego.

"The plans of the diligent lead to profit as surely as haste leads to poverty." Proverbs 21:5.

The Anchor for Success: Your Budget

Your financial boat must have an anchor and that is your budget. Without it, your boat will drift aimlessly and eventually sink. Please stop what you are doing right now and create a budget.

There are numerous easy templates and spreadsheets online. I personally use Dave Ramsey's Enemy of Debt. Block out at least an hour on your calendar to make your budget. **It's not hard, but it is absolutely essential to changing the way you view and manage your money. Little things add up, and you will quite likely be surprised to find how much you are spending on unnecessary things.** This is the starting point for every other financial goal in your life.

Tips for creating a monthly budget:

- Add up your income.
- Write down *everything* you spend in a month. Every. Single. Thing.
- Leave some padding for unexpected expenses, such as gifts, entertainment, repairs, and illness.
- Look for items to cut.
- Put all income and expenses in a spreadsheet or other template.

When you're done, print it and share it with your family. If you have children, talk to them about the family budget and work with them to create their own individual budgets as well. There are terrific templates for kids of all ages.

Finally, put ten minutes on your calendar at least twice a week to look at your budget and record your spending. Be diligent in this effort and you will see the payoff. You might even avoid costly overdraft fees. Reference your budget when you pay your monthly bills.

Small Changes Yield Big Results

One thing you'll probably notice right away in your budget is that you are spending a lot of money on unnecessary conveniences and indulgences—things like that four-dollar latte you pick up on the way to work every day, or that nine-dollar lunch salad you grab at the take-out place, or that thirty-five-dollar dinner at a restaurant every Friday night.

For one week, brew your own coffee, pack your lunch, and plan all dinners at home. Track your spending on your budget.

Here is one exercise my family tried, and it saved us a lot money: Our daughters swim in the morning from 5:30 to 7:30. They are ravenous after practice and love to have a Dunkin' Donuts breakfast sandwich and caramel latte (cost: almost eight dollars) or a Panera bagel sandwich and caramel macchiato (just over nine dollars). These are the costs in my community. I am sure they vary across the nation. Please understand, I think these products are terrific, but to spend this amount five mornings a week for both daughters, was costing us around ninety dollars per week! That's almost 4,000 dollars a year!

More Ways to Curb Overspending

A popular quote attributed to Will Rogers says, "Too many people spend money they haven't earned, to buy things they don't want, to impress people they don't like." I think the reason it's so popular is that it's so true. Think about it.

Before you purchase something, ask yourself why you're spending money on it and whether it is something you truly need or just something you want for reasons that don't serve your values or needs well. Ask yourself if the purchase is a good investment in your happiness and wellbeing.

"For where your treasure is, there your heart will be also." Matthew 6:21

It's fruitless to shame or blame yourself for buying lattes or bottled water. I cannot change the financially dumb things I have done in the past. But I now know how my guilty pleasures have sabotaged my budget. The hassle and wasted gas I have spent returning things I shouldn't have purchased in the first place could have bought me a share of Amazon stock.

But that's in the past. All you can change is your present and making changes now will change your future. So, don't feel guilty about the past, but do start controlling your spending now.

One way to do this is to know your real you when you shop. Even if something is stylish, that does not mean it looks good on you. It may not work for your lifestyle. Keep the tags on every piece of clothing you buy until you wear it. You may not like it as much when you see it on yourself at home or when you realize you have no place to wear it. Ask yourself if it is worth the price and the space in your closet. If not, return it.

Before you buy something, ask yourself if you truly need it or just want it. If it's the latter, don't buy it. Just because it looks cute on you doesn't mean you should buy it. Cut back on the wants and invest in the needs.

Shopping with friends is a great bonding experience, and a good friend can help you keep your spending in check. She will tell you those jeans are too tight or maybe ask you where and how many times you'll really wear that gorgeous but expensive party dress.

To curb overspending, it's also important not to use shopping as therapy. If you're feeling sad or stressed, instead of shopping, try exercising, reading, journaling, or any other free activity that you enjoy and find distracting.

Cost Per Use: A Lower Price Tag Isn't Always Cheaper

A five-dollar trendy t-shirt may seem financially responsible, but if it shrinks and loses its color in the first wash, the thirty-dollar basic one that fits you perfectly and lasts several years is probably a better spend. When the latest kitchen gadget or houseware item tempts you, ask yourself how many times you will use it and for what purpose—and answer honestly. If you'll only use it once or twice, it's probably not worth the expense or cupboard space it will take up.

Did you know you can borrow things like cake decorating equipment and other kitchen gadgets for free from your local library and online kitchen tool libraries? The website "Kitchen Share" (https://kitchenshare.org/) is a great resource.

The Value of a Spending Embargo

Every January for the last three years, I have had a shopping embargo where I do not purchase anything for myself until Easter. I have to stay away from the malls and my favorite discount retail stores. I am amazed at how much money is in my bank account when Easter rolls around.

The Debt Trap

Make no mistake: Debt costs you money. Period. Every time you take out a loan or carry a credit card balance, you are losing money. And the more debt you accumulate, the more it costs and the harder it is to get out of debt.

According to the 2017 State of Credit report by Experian, the average credit card debt in America is $5,000. That may not seem like much until you add the annual percentage rate interest charges. If you carry a balance of $5,000 for a year on a card with an APR of 14.9%, you will pay at least $745 in interest charges, possibly more, depending on whether the interest is compounded.

Compound interest is interest that is charged on the interest you owe in addition to the amount you charged originally. If you do not completely pay off your credit card balance every month, you could be losing hundreds and possibly thousands of dollars.

Just like admitting you may need to lose ten pounds, you might need to be ready to admit you have gained too many pounds in debt. Do everything you can to pay off your debt now, and then keep it paid off.

It's also important to know your credit score. Just like homework is graded on a scale of 0 to 100 by teachers, your financial habits are graded from 300 to 850 by your credit score. Your credit score is a three-digit number that predicts the likelihood you'll pay back a loan or credit card balance.

Your score is determined by evaluating your past financial behavior related to loans, credit cards and other bills. In other words, it evaluates your "credit worthiness," or whether or not a lender should approve you for a loan or credit card. If you have a low credit score, you will pay a higher interest rate—if you can get credit at all—because you are considered a poor risk.

Simplify! Purge! Consign! Give Away!

Take an hour a month to look at your clothing and accessories. Ask yourself these questions:

- Does this style and color flatter me?
- Does it fit well?
- Does it still work for my workplace or social activities?

If you answered no to any of these questions, give it away or consign it. If you haven't found a consignment store, find one. While they will take a percentage, most will give you discounts or credits to purchase items in their store. It is a great way to recycle and make some cash. There are also lots of online consignment stores online and in your neighborhood.

Additionally, there are countless women who need what you do not. Look locally for women's back-to-work programs, domestic violence shelters, churches, and homeless shelters. Many community colleges have women's back-to-work programs, and participants need new wardrobes and accessories when they start interviewing.

There is Such a Thing as Too Much Generosity

My godmother, Mignon, was the most generous and kind person the earth has seen. Mignon gave of her talents and treasures to everyone. Mignon never married, and we were her family. She and my mom were best friends and I don't remember any holiday, occasion, or even many meals without Mignon.

At Christmas, she would give and give and give. We often ran out of time and had to eat before opening all the presents. It was too much and while her love was genuine, it taught me a great deal about giving and getting.

I love to give gifts. Acknowledging a birthday, bringing a hostess gift to a party, and sending a happy box to a friend all bring joy to me. I keep a gift closet with special items to give away.

If you love giving gifts, it is easy to get carried away at Christmas and other giving holidays. But I'm here to tell you that you can be thoughtful without extravagance.

When my husband and I started our family, we made some tough decisions about gift giving. The one I am most proud of, which was difficult, was limiting our children to three gifts for Christmas. It was good enough for Jesus— the wise men brought him frankincense, gold, and myrrh— and it was good enough for our two daughters.

If you decide to try this, be ready. You may have guilt. Your children are terrific, just like mine. But they do not need an overabundance of things in their life.

When you feel like you have made the wrong decision, go to your local YMCA and ask about the Angel Tree program. You can pick children to give gifts to during the holidays. This is a ritual my family continues to enjoy. I hope you will experience it yourself. Some items these children have requested over the years: Ginny, age six, asked for a brush and lotion. James, age eight, asked for Snoopy sheets. Others asked for blankets, crayons, socks, and dolls. All such humble requests remind my family that we are blessed beyond measure.

Have an Emergency Fund and a Savings Account

When you stop overspending, you will have more money to save, and you should start saving right now. Most financial experts suggest you need a cash stash large enough to pay for six months of expenses: If you need $5,000 to survive every month, save $30,000. Personal finance guru Suze Orman advises an eight-month emergency fund because that's about how long it takes the average person to find a job.

Create a separate free savings account and put money in it automatically every month. This savings account is different from an emergency fund. Your emergency fund pays your everyday living expenses if you lose your job or become unable to work. The savings account pays for unexpected expenses like car repairs, household appliance replacements, even medical bills.

Insurance

Once you stop overspending on things you don't need, you can afford to buy things you do need, things that will assure your financial stability and protect you from disaster. Insurance is one of those things.

This could be a full book in itself. In addition to having the essential coverage—health, car, and home—you should explore other kinds of insurance as well. If you are employed, you should have life, accidental, disability, and perhaps other types of insurance.

If you are self-employed, retired, or even unemployed, you still need these to make sure you and your family are protected. Terms and circumstances are different for everyone. I encourage you to explore these crucial policies: life, disability, and long-term care insurance. Research and seek financial experts to help you select the options that are right for you.

Prepare for Retirement

In addition to an emergency fund and a savings account for unexpected expense, you need to prepare for the time when you will no longer have to or be able to work. The sooner you start, the more comfortable and secure you will be, and the more likely you will be able to quit working when you reach retirement age. That Social Security check that awaits you is not intended to fully support you, and it won't.

If you want to be able to actually retire and live comfortably, start saving money in a tax-deferred retirement account immediately. Not next week. Not when you get a raise. Not next year. Not tomorrow. *Today!* Your retirement money is meant to support you when you no longer work full-time so that you can enjoy the fruits of your lifelong labor. It is not meant to bail you out of stupid mistakes. We all make them, and I have made many.

Familiarize yourself with retirement options such as **401k, SEP, IRA and other tools.**

Here's the rule of thumb amount you need to be saving for retirement. By your thirtieth birthday, you should have banked half the amount of your annual salary. For example, if you're making $50,000 a year, you should have banked $25,000 by your thirtieth birthday. By age forty, you should have twice your annual salary. By age fifty, four times your salary, by age sixty, six times, and by age sixty-seven, eight times. That means that on your sixty-seventh birthday, if your annual salary is $75,000, you should have $600,000 saved.

Don't give in to the temptation to cash out your retirement account early. If you take money out of your retirement account, you will have to pay taxes on it and possibly pay an early withdrawal penalty of ten percent. That means if you take $50,000 out of your retirement account, you could end up paying $15,000 or more!

Investing

Once you put yourself on a budget, stop overspending, and start saving, you're ready to make your money work for you. Wise investing will make your money multiply and give you more wealth and security in the future, especially in retirement. The sooner you start investing, the more money you will end up with, so start now, even if you have only a small amount to invest.

According to the 2018 Fidelity Women and Investing Study, women are good at investing. Additionally, women own more diverse portfolios, trade less often, incur fewer fees, and are less likely to panic sell in a downturn than men. According to studies, these smart moves mean that women annually earn between 0.4% and one percent more than men. This can result in twelve percent larger retirement nest eggs for women over a thirty-year period. The younger you are, the higher the likelihood you will be wealthier if you've created and maintained a savings and investing plan.

Don't let lack of knowledge stop you. A good certified financial planner can help you set up an investment plan. Just as you would when you're looking for a great doctor, hair dresser, babysitter, or trainer, you need to do your homework. This person is part of your financial village, along with a good accountant and good banker. Select someone who is competent and ethical, has a proven track record and practices what they preach.

Finding the Willpower to Change

The "marshmallow experiment" begun in the 1960s by psychologist Walter Mischel provides great lessons on willpower. He offered four-year-old children the choice of a marshmallow now, or two if they could wait fifteen minutes. Researchers tracked the performance of these children as they became adults. They found that children who resisted immediate temptation in favor of a greater delayed payoff achieved greater academic success, better health, and lower rates of marital separation and divorce.

In a second study, 1,000 children were tracked using the marshmallow experiment from birth to the age of thirty-two. The researchers found that childhood self-control predicted better outcomes in physical health, substance dependence, personal finances, and criminal offenses. This was true even when other factors such as intelligence and social class were considered. They even compared sibling pairs and found that the sibling in each pair with lower self-control had poorer outcomes, despite shared family background.

So how do you find the willpower to exercise self-control and make the changes I've suggested in this chapter? It's important to know that making these changes does not mean you are depriving yourself of anything. In fact, if you start making these changes today, you will have more independence, more money, more self-confidence and more peace of mind in the future. You will have the ability to purchase what you truly need and what truly makes you happy.

I hope you learned valuable lessons this week and kept your journal of must-dos. Reflect on some thoughts here and maybe put them on your to-do list for becoming women wi$e.

WEEK 4

REFILL YOUR BUCKET

"Be on your guard; stand firm in the faith; be coura-geous; be strong." 1 Corinthians 16:13

Day 1

Of the many confident and courageous women in the Bible, Esther stands out. The story is inspiring as we see a woman of principle putting others before herself. Read the book of Esther from the Old Testament and write notes below where Esther was confident, courageous, and well spoken.

_____

_____

_____

Day 2

Now that you have read the entire book, record three verses where Esther was confident. Where do you see the refer-ence to twelve and the introduction to maybe a "spa"? Hint Chapter 2:8-9. I love the Bible!

_____

_____

_____

Relate these verses to a time when you felt confident.

_____

_____

_____

Day 3

Look back at your notes, record three verses where Esther was courageous.

_____

_____

_____

Relate these verses to a time when you felt courageous.

_____

_____

_____

Day 4

Looking back at your notes and references in the book of Esther, record three verses where she was well-spoken. Look at the way she goes about asking the king to free her people. That is WOW (women of wisdom). How about her bravery when she says, "I will fast for three days and three nights. If I perish, I perish"?

_____

_____

_____

Relate these verses to a time when you were well-spoken.

_____

_____

_____

Day 5
Value Assessment Day

What did you learn about your values this month? Look back at your notes from the last few weeks. Are you confident, courageous, well-spoken, well-read, and financially smart? If these are already your values, describe what areas you need to grow. Which of these values do not resonate with you? Is there another value that surfaced for you? If so, describe it.

_____

_____

_____

_____

_____

_____

_____

_____

_____

_____

_____

BE CURIOUS

What is Your Superpower?

BE Curious

"I have no special talent, I am only passionately curious." Albert Einstein

You may not drive a tricked-out bat mobile or fly an invisible airplane, but I know you are a super hero. Wonder Woman has been my all-time favorite character since I was five. Really, those bracelets that repel bullets, arriving in an invisible plane and that gold lasso of truth—what else do we need? I know you balance demands and schedules with superhuman endurance. And, I bet you wish on a few occasions when you showed up in the same dress or wrong dress to an event, you wish you were invisible. You have traces of super powers and here is one more to add. Curiosity. It starts with asking, "Why?"

Today's culture has countless ways to obtain facts and information. Turn off the loud noises of Twitter, Facebook, and Instagram and turn on your curiosity and creativity. Too many women today are letting others' beliefs become their own. Be curious and relearn how to critically think.

We cannot be curious when we are only listening to other's voices. We need to think critically by asking questions to discover new information. The ultimate cheat sheet to expand our critical thinking and curiosity skills is to ask: Who? What? Where? When? Why? How?

Curiosity has been proven to increase intelligence, problem solving skills, creativity, and improve learning and memory. We are born curious and somewhere along the way, usually when we begin school, the answers become more important than the question. Stephanie Vozza's article, *Eight Habits of Curious People*, published in Fast Company, listed these traits. Curious people:

- Listen without judgment
- Ask lots of questions
- Seek surprise
- Are fully present
- Are willing to be wrong
- Make time for curiosity
- Are willing to say "I don't know"
- Don't let past hurts affect the future

BE interesting, interested, and creative.

WEEK 1

BE INTERESTED

Be gracious in your speech. The goal is to bring out the best in others in a conversation, not to put them down, not to cut them out. Colossians 4:6

I LOVE BOOKS AND READING TIME WAS ONE OF my favorite moments with our daughters when they were growing up. The joy as they selected their book, cuddled in my lap and read or listened, gave me a bright light into their heart. I learned when we express interest in children or adults, they are refreshed with hope and confidence. When we pay attention to someone's skills, they are usually empowered to develop those skills. Watch what happens each time a coach focuses on a young athlete, or a teacher seeks out a quiet student with special skills, or a boss highlights the talents of an employee. You will see a refreshed sense of focus along with more motivation from the recipient of the attention.

Being interested in others builds strong relationships. Relationships build a BEtter you. Listening with an open heart and open mind has been the single most important action I can take when building and sustaining relationships. This week we are going to spend time practicing values that build our superpowers.

Day 1

"You will show me the path of life; in your presence is fulness of joy; At your right hand are pleasures forevermore." Psalm 16:11

YOU WILL LEARN SO MUCH MORE ABOUT A person or topic if you listen without judgment. Today, ask four questions of at least four people. Write down the questions and the person below and don't let the answer be more important than the question. You will be delighted what you might learn about a friend, co-worker, spouse, or family member. Who needs you to BE interested in them today and how will you be engaged?

_____

_____

_____

_____

_____

_____

_____

_____

Prayer:

_____

Grateful Gift

_____

DAY 2

"Each of you should look not only to your own interests but to those of others." Philippians 2:4

MY RESEARCH AND PREPARATION FOR BE 12 included gaining wisdom from countless women of all walks of life. These lovely ladies shared how their value system led to their success. They shared stories of their highs and lows, the loneliness and the joys. These women were bank executives, physicians, single moms, widowers, and cancer survivors, to name a few. Tracy is an example of a grounded, focused friend who rose to leadership in the Professional Golf Association, a male dominated organization. As the tournament director for one of the PGAs largest golf tournaments, Tracy credits her values of confidence, hard work and advocating for herself as critical.

Arlene is another example of a woman who lives and shares them to develop other women. She served in leadership under several Florida Governors. She focused on putting women in state advocacy positions. She leads a wildly successful company and is the national director for the Florida Women's Conference. Did I mention, all while going to dialysis? She puts the interests of women before herself daily.

Who needs to hear from you today? Find an interesting piece of information or news to share with someone. Is there a friend, family member, client, or prospect, who may be trying to lose weight, learn a new skill, or another who's interested in a trip to an exotic place? How will you show your interest in them?

_____

_____

_____

_____

_____

_____

_____

_____

_____

_____

_____

_____

_____

_____

_____

_____

Prayer:

_____

Grateful Gift:

_____

DAY 3

"To put off your old self, which belongs to your former manner of life and is corrupt through deceitful desires and to be renewed in the spirit of your minds. And to put on the new self, created after the likeness of God in true righteousness and holiness." Ephesians 4:22-24

I REFER TO MY "OLD SELF" OFTEN. I DIDN'T always like that girl who was busy multi-tasking and trying to be all things to all people. I missed many opportunities to serve. For years, I was caught up with being super mom, perfect wife, and great boss—all with a smile on my face. I gave up friends by making poor choices. I missed birthdays and celebrations. I didn't stand for anything, so I fell for a lot. I went from meeting to meeting, business travel, conferences, and taking on more tasks that I should. I have more than once put lotion on my hair and conditioner on my legs. I have mistaken mascara for lipstick when frantically going from one task to another. I am embarrassed to say I was stuck in the quicksand, believing my importance and success depended on how busy I was. I broke busy and kicked her to the curb. It was painful, but that life did not reflect my values and who I was created to BE.

What can you take off your plate today to show your interest in those around you? How will you remove the urge to multi-task or not listen to the answers when you ask the questions? Who needs your attention today? Today, ask lots of questions and write down what you learned about others. How can you BE less busy and more interested in others?

_____

_____

_____

_____

_____

_____

_____

_____

_____

_____

_____

_____

_____

_____

_____

Prayer:

_____

Grateful Gift:

_____

DAY 4

"Pride goes before destruction and a haughty spirit before a fall." Proverbs 16:18

TODAY BE OPEN AND CURIOUS WITHOUT BEING invested in the outcome, and be willing to be wrong. Is there a situation or topic you struggle with that is preventing you from gaining all the facts? There are six words that can strengthen a relationship and build trust. "I was wrong. I am sorry." We all sin. Confess and move to BEing your BEst.

Are you willing to BE wrong? With whom? Share the situation. Maybe someone needs to hear, "I am sorry."

_____

_____

_____

_____

_____

_____

_____

Prayer:

_____

Grateful Gift:

_____

Day 5

"An unfriendly person pursues selfish ends and against all sound judgment starts quarrels." Proverbs 18:1

THE SELFISH SOUL CAN REAR ITS HEAD WHEN least expected. Perhaps it is when you're telling half the story or hoarding your treasures from someone who needs them. To be concerned with only ourselves is not how God designed us. He created us to give with a great heart. What humble qualities do you possess? Who are some of the most unselfish people you know and what are their qualities?

_____

_____

_____

_____

_____

_____

_____

_____

_____

Prayer:

_____

Grateful Gift:

_____

Week 2

BE Interesting

We are the clay, you are the potter: we are all the work of your hand." Isaiah 64:8

The world is your oyster, and you are the pearl. Pearls are beautiful yet born of an irritant that makes its way into the oyster's shell. Scientists disagree about whether it's sand or not, but it irritates the interior of the shell and over time a pearl is formed. We are becoming pearls every day as we tackle challenges that get inside and irritate us.

You are likely asking yourself, what does this have to do with interesting. I love facts, trivia and sharing them with others as I build relationships.

There are many random facts that I find interesting, and I value interesting people because they help me grow. Interesting people have perspective, authenticity and connection. They have a good sense of humor. I desire to reflect those values.

Here are twelve interesting facts, as rated by www.list. com and found on Google, that you may want to share with others.

1. Giraffes can clean their ears with their tongues.
2. Creative people remember vivid dreams better.

3.   Russia considered beer a soft drink until 2011.
4. The height of the Eiffel Tower changes with the temperature.
5. You can't hum with your nose closed.
6. The cat is the only domestic animal not mentioned in the Bible.
7. A bee sting can relieve arthritis pain.
8. In 1968 "#" was called an 'octothorp' as a joke.
9. Americans eat 100 acres of pizza a day.
10. The Bible is about 611,000 words long.
11. The book of James is the bossiest book of the Bible. And a favorite of mine.
12. The tongue is the strongest muscle in the body. Use it wisely and lovingly.

I share these with you for a giggle and to remind you to seek out fun, unique and fascinating facts to share with others. You may find it helps you grow and builds relationships along the way.

DAY 1

"For God hath not given us the spirit of fear, but of power, and of love and of a sound mind."
2 Timothy 1:7

News around the world is often difficult to read. Senseless killings, brutality, abuse, and greed—just to name a few. Instead of allowing it to consume me in a negative way, I use the daily news to spread joy. Each day I find a piece of news or information where God is present and pass it on. What can you find today that will send a bright light to someone?

_____

_____

_____

_____

_____

Prayer:

_____

Grateful Gift:

_____

Day 2

"If you need wisdom, ask our generous God, and he will give it to you. He will not rebuke you for asking." James 1:5

I AM A JACK OF ALL TRADES AND MASTER OF some. In order for me to be respected in my field, at work and at home, I need knowledge. How can you become the expert? What knowledge do you need to BE more confident in your work or personal expertise and to BE more interesting? Is there a conference, blog, daily news feed, or book that will give you wisdom?

_____

_____

_____

_____

_____

_____

_____

_____

Prayer:

_____

Grateful Gift:

_____

Day 3

"I have put the words in your mouth." Jeremiah 1:9b

LEARN HOW TO TELL A GOOD STORY. THINK about your childhood, college, your first job, travels, and experiences. Write down at least one story. If you cannot think of one, you can retell one of the top parables from the Bible. Open your Bible and take a good read.

Matthew 25:14-30: The Talents
Mark 4:30-32: The Mustard Seed
Luke 15:3-7: The Lost Sheep
Luke 10:25-37: The Good Samaritan
Luke 15:11-32: The Prodigal Son
Matthew 5:14-15: Light of the World
Luke 6:46-49: Wise Builders
Matthew 13:3-23: The Seed and Types of Soil
Jeremiah 18:1-10: The Potter

Which one was your favorite? Why? Which one (s) will you retell? And to whom? Tell a story below.

_____

_____

_____

_____

_____

_____

_____

_____

_____

_____

_____

_____

_____

_____

_____

_____

_____

_____

_____

_____

_____

_____

Prayer:

_____

Grateful Gift:

_____

_____

DAY 4

"You have made known to me the paths of life; you will fill me with joy in your presence." Acts 2:28

WHAT DO YOU BRING TO THE TABLE TODAY that is beyond basic skills and knowledge? In three to five sentences, describe how you are creative and interesting.

_____

_____

_____

_____

_____

_____

_____

_____

_____

_____

_____

_____

_____

Prayer:

_____

Grateful Gift:

_____

DAY 5

CURIOSITY IS A SUPERPOWER. TODAY, REFER TO yourself as "Captain Curious" and be humble enough to say, "I don't know." Now, find the answer to what you don't know. Seek out people today that are doing something you aren't familiar with and find ways to engage. Describe how it helped you BE more interesting.

_____

_____

_____

_____

_____

_____

_____

_____

_____

_____

_____

_____

Prayer:

_____

Grateful Gift:

WEEK 3

BE CREATIVE

"The journey of a thousand miles begins with one step." Lao-Tzu

WHAT IS CREATIVITY, ANYWAY? IT IS A WAY OF life that embraces **originality and mixes discipline, knowledge, and imagination.** As of today, you are no longer allowed to say, "I am not creative." I have seen "non-creative" people plan a fundraiser, coordinate a car pool, create a marvelous meal from scratch, plant a beautiful garden, and solve a major crisis.

Creativity can be learned, and it can be improved. In the 1960s, NASA approached researcher George Land for an instrument to measure its most creative employees. He and his team developed a tool and were so intrigued when it worked that they applied it to children. They conducted additional research on 1,600 kids at five, ten, and fifteen years old to determine the genius category of creativity. They discovered that at five years of age, ninety-eight percent were creative. It declined to thirty percent at age ten and twelve percent at age fifteen. Instead of seeing this as bad news, BE the change and treat creativity like a muscle. Work it!

This week, develop and exercise it. We can be creative by experiencing, asking questions, exploring, and using our imagination. *Harvard Business Review*, October 1998, outlined three components of creativity. They are **expertise, creative thinking, and motivation**. Expertise includes knowledge and intellectual proficiency. Creative thinking requires skills and imagination. Intrinsic and extrinsic motivation is influenced by our environments and provides tangible rewards. We will use all three of these to BEcome more creative this week.

DAY 1

"Let the heavens rejoice, let the earth be glad; let the sea resound, and all that is in it. Let the fields be jubilant, and everything in them; let all the trees of the forest sing for joy." Psalm 96:11-1

EXPERIMENT AND EXPLORE. LOOK OUTSIDE.
Take ten minutes, lie flat outside, and look at the clouds. Listen to what you hear. Think about what you see. Describe with deep creativity what you see and hear and how it makes you feel.

_____

_____

_____

_____

_____

_____

_____

_____

_____

Prayer:

_____

Grateful Gift:

_____

DAY 2

"Imagination is more important than knowledge. Knowledge is limited, whereas imaginations embraces the entire world, stimulating progress, giving birth to evolution." Albert Einstein

DO YOU REMEMBER THE DISNEY CHARACTER, Figment? He was an adorable purple dinosaur-looking character. I have one sitting on my desk to remind me to imagine the possibilities. My godmother, Mignon, often referred to Figment to encourage me to get out of my box, stretch my comfort zone, and to calm me when I was scared. Whether it was the monster in the closet or the Sunday night tears about going back to school, Mignon reminded me, "It's a figment of your imagination."

Are you stuck in the daily grind or are you ready to imagine new possibilities? Think of a situation, problem, or opportunity you are in right now. Maybe it is a conversation you need to have with someone. Embrace your imagination as you find solutions. Describe in detail how thinking out of the box helped the situation.

_____

_____

Prayer:

_____

Grateful gift:

_____

DAY 3

"You make known to me the path of life; you will fill me with joy in your presence, with eternal pleasures at your right hand." Psalm 16:11

IN ORDER TO BE WHOLE BRAINED, WE NEED TO think convergently and divergently. Divergent thinking stimulates ideas and uses countless ways to reach a solution. It requires imagination and generating new possibilities. Convergent thinking seeks the final solution using facts to reach the answer.

Think divergently today as you consider twenty ways to improve a common object. It can be shoes, a stove, a car, food—whatever you want.

_____

_____

_____

_____

_____

_____

_____

Prayer:

_____

Grateful gift:

_____

Day 4

Be brave enough to live life creatively. The creative is the place where no one else has ever been. You have to leave the city of your comfort and go into the wilderness of your intuition. You can't get there by bus, only by hard work and risk and by not quite knowing what you're doing. What you'll discover will be wonderful. What you'll discover will be yourself. Carla Harris, Expect to Win: 10 Proven Strategies for Thriving in the Workplace

DISSECT THIS QUOTE BY CARLA HARRIS, AND read any of her books to learn about one of the most fascinating, accomplished women of our time. Leave your comfort zone and write down what you have learned about creativity. If you BElieve in its value, how can you BEcome more creative?

_____

_____

_____

_____

Prayer:

_____

Grateful gift:

_____

Day 5

READ EXODUS 35:30-33 AND LOOK AT THE skills God gave Bezalel and write them below. Today is the day to put your creativity to work. Here are some ideas you can do alone or with family or friends. Get a white board and just draw, design a dream house, finger-paint a sunset, cut out a collage of your favorite things, word art adjectives and affirmations, paint, or find a clay or pottery class. The options are endless.

_____

_____

_____

_____

_____

_____

_____

_____

_____

Prayer:

_____

Grateful Gift:

_____

Week 4

Reach For Your Cape

My daddy, Jim, was my superhero. He was eternally optimistic, faithful, relational, and fun. He meticulously planned an annual family summer retreat at Barkley Lake and the Catlett Christmas. Uncles, aunts, cousins, and friends were all welcome. Every year, around the July Fourth weekend, we gathered for countless hours of swimming, fishing, skiing, eating, and all the trouble we could find. Then, in December, Daddy gathered the gang for the Catlett Christmas, a holiday celebration with amazing southern cooking, stories, and laughter. The Catlett Clan etched values into my fiber that remain today.

When my father was diagnosed with Pick's Disease, I was devastated. I went through all the phases when tragedy strikes. Denial was first. Then questioning, guilt, and anger quickly followed. I soon became obsessed with learning more about the brain, not just his disease. The three years we had with him taught hard lessons about living and dying. There were devastating and heartbreaking moments. But there is light in all darkness. Throughout his illness, my sister Michele and I stuck together and rallied during tough times. We spent the last few days with Daddy curled up on a couch in the hospice facility. We laughed and cried as we recounted the blessings of a life well lived.

Heroes show up in tragic moments. The time with Michele and the months that followed reminded me of my sister's superpowers. She is smart, loyal, driven, and always "has my back."

BE a sister, and guard those you love. Also, it doesn't hurt to remind your heroes how much you value them.

What I learned about the brain during this period prompted me to pick these values for this month. We have to treat our brain like a muscle. As we wrap up this month, let's look at your superpowers of listening, learning, and being creative.

Day 1
What did you create last week? Was it a painting, a sketch? Did you go to a museum? Take pictures of a sunset? Describe your emotions when you were creating. Take a picture of what you created and share it with someone.

Day 2
Daily, I work to refine my listening skills. BEing interested in others is a simple way to connect and let people know they are important. I have found this phrase to be most helpful: "Tell me what you mean by that." Try asking this question, and listen for the answers. Describe tricks you use to listen better. What did you learn about someone else today when you truly listened?

_____

_____

_____

Day 3

BE interested in someone for the rest of this week. Give full attention to either a child, spouse, or coworker. Find a skill in which they are proficient or one that might need a bit of refining. Watch the miracles happen, and write about the renewed hope and confidence you see.

_____

_____

_____

Day 4

Jesus' mother, Mary, was a heroine with God-given powers. First, she had joy in an unbelievable situation. Read Luke 1:26-56. In this passage, you read Mary's prayer of glory and praise after an angel tells her she will have a son. She remained peaceful when serving as Jesus' mother. She watched her son be ridiculed, beaten, and crucified. Think about Mary's life and list her powers.

_____

_____

_____

Day 5
Value Assessment Day
Today is your day of reflection. Look back on your notes. Describe your BE moments of this past month. What did you learn about BEing interested, interesting, and creative? What cape are you going to wear?

_____

_____

_____

_____

_____

_____

BE DISCIPLINED

Decisions, Not Circumstances, Determine Your Destiny

BE Disciplined

"Whoever loves discipline loves knowledge, but whoever hates correction is ignorant." Proverbs 12:1

OUR DAUGHTERS, MEGAN AND MOLLY, ARE swimmers and define discipline. Their typical day includes rising at 5 am and swimming until school begins. They swim after school, do homework, eat, sleep, repeat. And they would tell you it's worth the work for a few seconds of improvement. Unlike football or soccer, when you might score the winning goal, shaving six seconds off 100 Butterfly is a large feat. The sacrifices of vacations, green hair from the chlorine, missing friend events, and being sore and tired have been great. Their decisions have helped to form their future.

BEing disciplined is the bridge between goals and accomplishments, winning or losing. It builds confidence and if we do not have self-control that comes from discipline, we will BE slaves to what controls us. Forty percent of our behavior is habit-driven, so if you want to control your ability to be self-disciplined, control your habits.

"For the Spirit God gave us does not make us timid, but gives us power, love and self-discipline." 2 Timothy 1:7

Self-discipline is the biggest obstacle stopping people from reaching the success they desire. It takes power to set your goal, prioritize, stay focused, and follow through to completion. Writing this book could have been the most focused I have been on any one project. There were many days I doubted my skills and fought negative self-talk. Instead of allowing fear to own me, I embraced carpe diem as I seized every day as a new opportunity to build habits of self-discipline and grit.

God's laws require us to BE disciplined. His first and most important commandment is to love Him with all your heart. The second is to love our neighbors as ourselves. Additionally, He gave us the Ten Commandments from Exodus 20:2-17. You have likely heard countless sermons on these and today, I challenge you to take a new look at them and ask yourself just a few questions about BEing disciplined.

1. I am the Lord your God, who brought you out of the land of Egypt. You shall have no other gods before me. **BE loyal.** God reminds us that developing and maintaining a true and active relationship with Him is the most important commitment we will ever make. Money, work, exercise, food, friends or family cannot go before our worship to God.
2. You shall not worship any other god. **BE committed.** God made us in His likeness.
3. You shall not take the name of the Lord your God in vain.

BE reverent. Respect is the cornerstone of every relationship. While it may be culturally common, we should not use our speech or actions to dishonor God.

4. Remember the Sabbath day to keep it holy.
   BE restful. Set time to focus on God and be rejuvenated.

5. Honor your father and mother.
   BE honorable. Families may be fractured and flawed, yet God's commandment calls for respect for parental authority.

6. You shall not murder.
   BE in harmony with others. God calls us to demonstrate love, not hate.

7. You shall not commit adultery.
   BE pure in your relationships. In an age of infidelity, God commands us to demonstrate our love for the partner we have chosen in marriage by not having sexual relations with another.

8. You shall not steal.
   BE satisfied. God wants us to prosper, but not by taking what is not ours.

9. You shall not bear false witness against your neighbor.
   BE honest. Just as we discussed in our first week, everything in the life of a Christian is anchored in truth.

10. You shall not covet.
    BE content. Look at yourself and your life and be fulfilled and gratified by what God has given you. Wanting what others have can entrap us to deeper sin.

BE a hard worker, goal minded and prepared.

Week 1

BE a Hard Worker

"Whatever you do, work at it with all your heart, as working for the Lord, not for men." Colossians 3:23

If talent counts once, effort counts twice. I believe most of what we do is ninety-nine percent perspiration and that you should love what you do and do what you love. Yet, it is never that easy.

Because one of my strengths is Futuristic, I have dreamed many careers paths. At age seven, I was obsessed with being an astronaut. I read about space and space travelers every chance I could. What I didn't know, was that I *could* have been an astronaut. Yes, I well understand the odds. But in fifth grade, I had a teacher who "told" me I couldn't.

This story plays out around us every day. If you were told you weren't good enough, may the journaling you have been doing for the last several months prove to you that you can BE anything. God made you perfect in His eyes.

My family taught me the value of hard work. My parents were divorced when I was four so I don't recall my father living in the house. What I remember was a mother and father that worked hard to give me the tools to succeed. While they didn't love each other, they loved my sister and me. My mother went to school and became a nurse. I watched her study hard, graduate, and work night shifts so she could be with us during the day. I also had a village of loving friends and family that supported me. My Aunt Ruth and Uncle Billy, Mignon, my grandfather, and friends worked tirelessly to make sure we had roots to grow and wings to fly.

Making a life versus making a living is a choice we make. My choice was clear: I had to work hard to make the life I wanted. I started working when I was fourteen by mowing lawns, babysitting, waitressing, and worked in the summers for government organizations and other odd jobs. After graduating from Centre College, my first real job was in banking. My goal was to be in healthcare and my dad urged me to learn business first. After Sean and I married and moved to Orlando, I left banking. I did not have a job so I started going door-to-door meeting with hospital executives. I identified the top organizations, their leadership, and then would call or drop by their office for an appointment. This may sound old fashioned, but email wasn't the first form of communication in 1995. I learned so much by visiting with these experts and with God's grace, two gentleman, Bob Kodzis and John Hillenmeyer, took my call later became my bosses and mentors. I was blessed to start my career with one of Florida's largest and most respected healthcare systems, Orlando Health. The biggest lesson I learned during this season was the power of relationships. Relationships require focus, dedication, and commitment.

We all need a village, and I found one as I began my second career. In 1997, I was riding home with what would later become a true gal pal. Shannon was a lobbyist for one of the world's largest companies, and frankly, my idol. She was beautiful, funny, and had the coolest job. I will admit, this chick from Kentucky thought the lobby was a northern term for foyer. And lobbying, what was that? Who would have thought, twenty years later, I would be telling a story about an amazing career in advocacy? I learned to be an advocate from the best in the field. My village grew to other lobbyists, hospital presidents, senators, representatives, and other elected and appointed officials.

There is a village waiting for you if you are humble enough to ask and then listen to wise advise.

Day 1

*"There is nothing better for a person than that he
should eat and drink and find enjoyment in his toil."
Ecclesiastes 2:24*

ANGELA DUCKWORTH'S BESTSELLER, *GRIT,* IS
inspiring. "Grit" is perseverance and passion. My old self
looked for shortcuts until I realized the hard problems are
the most rewarding.

Think back to algebra, chemistry, or any problem that
you had to use steps to work out. We should apply that same
rigor to BEcoming excellent. You know, excellence is defined
by you, not anyone else. Take the Grit test and talk about
your score at http://angeladuckworth.com/grit-scale/

_____

_____

_____

_____

_____

_____

_____

Prayer:
_____

Grateful gift:
_____

Day 2

"When people fall down, do they not get up?"
Jeremiah 8:4a

I BELIEVE IN FAILURE. I HAVE DONE IT BIG AND bad and learned valuable lessons every time. Whether it was moving to a new job that wasn't the right fit or saying something hurtful, God will continue to give us successes and failure.

How do you define success? Success for me is the ability to create the life I want.

Describe failures that have pushed you to greatness.

_____

_____

_____

_____

_____

_____

_____

_____

Prayer:

_____

Grateful gift:

_____

Day 3

"Commit your work to the Lord and your plans will be established." Proverbs 16:3

FINALLY, AT 50, I BELIEVE THIS. IN MY LOST year, I doubted God would establish my plans. Yet, I was still in control. Now, I start every day with this verse. Every work I do, whether fixing my family dinner, presenting solutions to a client, giving a speech, or serving the homeless, is the work I commit to the Lord.

Describe how you will commit your work to the Lord. Once you do, sit back and watch how the plans are established.

_____

_____

_____

_____

_____

_____

_____

_____

Prayer:

_____

Grateful gift:

_____

Day 4

"No temptation has overtaken you except what is common to man. And God is faithful; he will not let you be tempted beyond what you can bear. But when you are tempted, he will also provide a way for you to endure it." 1 Corinthians 10:13

TEMPTATION LOOKS DIFFERENT EVERY DAY. Think about what tempts you. Is it gossiping, coveting, lying, laziness, calling in late to play hooky? This Scripture promises that God will provide a way out. He will lead your lips to silence when we want to say something hurtful or untrue. Describe a time when you were tempted and how did God intervene and give you a way to endure.

_____

_____

_____

_____

_____

_____

_____

Prayer:

_____

Grateful gift:

_____

Day 5

"The heart of man plans his way, but the Lord establishes his steps." Proverbs 16:9

READ PROVERBS 19:20 AND DESCRIBE WHAT IT says about BEcoming wise. You can seek wisdom by asking for it from wise counsel. Then be disciplined to listen and apply the knowledge you have obtained. What plans are in your heart or mind that need your hard work and determination to succeed? Whether it is your career, volunteer, or a project, write down if you are truly working hard and if not, what do you need to do to reach success?

_____

_____

_____

_____

_____

_____

_____

_____

Prayer:

_____

Grateful gift:

Week 2

BE Goal-Minded

"Set your hearts on things above ... Set your minds on things above, not on earthly things." Colossians 3:1b-2

Goals are plans and commitments to achieve a desired endpoint. They are the wind in our sails and the rudder guiding our boat. They give us focus and direction, keep us motivated, and help us vision the future we desire.

When I wrote down my goals for writing this book, I had no idea what the future held. I wanted to give up many times. The hours spent on this book required a focus that only God could deliver. Remember: focus is not my strongest skill. I relied on prayers and encouragement from others. I kept 'looking up' for God to keep me focused. Beginning with the end in mind and keeping my written goals where I could see them every day, gave me the strength to prevail.

You either have the grit to achieve goals or you do not. You can make excuses, blame circumstances, or give up. The feeling of achieving a goal is unmatched. May this week be rewarding as you evaluate what goals really mean to BEing your BEst.

Day 1

"I know the plans I have for you." Jeremiah 29:11

TODAY TAKE THE TIME TO SET GOALS FOR yourself. If you already have at least three personal and three professional goals, then use this time to write them down again. Are they SMART? If you have not written down your personal and professional/family goals, now is the time. And, find an accountability partner with whom you can share your goals, struggles and wins. Develop a system to regularly check in as you encourage each other. Write down your goals using the SMART technique and write down the names of those people who will encourage you.

1. Set goals that motivate you.
2. **S**pecific. **M**easurable. **A**ttainable. **R**elevant. **T**ime-bound.
3. Write it down.
4. Make an action plan.
5. Stick with it.

_____

_____

_____

_____

_____

Prayer:

_____

Grateful gift:

_____

DAY 2

Read Luke14:28-31. How do these verses give us tips on setting goals?

_____

_____

_____

JOHN DOERR, IN HIS BOOK, *MEASURE WHAT Matters,* describes his Objectives, Key Results (OKR) model. His model has been used to help some of the world's best companies achieve their goals. This framework outlines critical thinking and discipline. The secret is to only have a few objectives and to focus on the results. Too often, organizations, people, and families have so many objectives that we cannot focus on any.

Look at the goals you wrote down yesterday. Below write down at least two objectives and key results beside each goal. What can you do today to focus on that goal? What do you need to do this week and this month to achieve the objectives you have listed?

_____

_____

_____

_____

_____

_____

_____

_____

_____

Prayer:

_____

Grateful gift:

_____

Day 3

*"Trust in the Lord with all your heart and lean not on
your own understanding; in all your ways acknowledge him, and he will make your paths straight."*
Proverbs 3:5-6

SETTING GOALS IS HARD AND WORKING TO
achieve them is even harder. It takes self-control and strength
not to crumble. It takes grit and the ability to manage your
expectations. Your goals are exactly that: yours. Please do
not be disappointed when others don't throw you a party
when you have reached a goal. They don't love you any less
when they aren't jumping for joy when you submitted your
manuscript. And this should not stop you from *celebrating*!

Sister, you create your own happiness and when you
reach your goals, *celebrate*. What actions do you need to
take to meet the goals you have set for yourself? Do you
need to trust God more? If yes, have you asked Him to
help? Think about your village. Do you have everyone you
need to help you achieve these goals? If not, what are you
going to do to add those people to your village?

Prayer:

_____

Grateful gift:

_____

Day 4

From everyone who had been given much, much will be demanded; and from the one who has been entrusted with much, much more will be asked."
Luke 12:48

THE SECOND COMPANY I STARTED, SHAMROX USA, was the result of something I had dreamed of for years. I am passionate about causes, women and my country. Shamrox was a sports clothing line with yoga wear and the pocket bra. Like any entrepreneur, I was clueless at first, worked hard and sought wisdom from others. I didn't know how to sew on a button. I was working full-time, had two daughters under five, and was pursuing my MBA. It started with an idea and then I was like a dog with a bone teaching myself about the clothing industry. My goals centered around sportswear designed for women by women, made in the USA with all proceeds going toward children's healthcare. I am proud to report, I met my goals.

I created it to be a cause-related company with its proceeds going to children's health initiatives. I wrote down all the goals and began assembling the village: designers, pattern makers, material, and manufacturers. Many men told me I had to go offshore because I could never make it in the US. Yet, if I ever heard "no," I knew I must not be asking the question right. God delivered a female pattern maker and seamstress and they were all within an hour of my home. God is so *great*! No dream is too small or goal too hard to achieve.

Rewrite two of your three goals. Who do you need in your universe to help you achieve it? What are you going to do to invite and empower them to help you meet your goals?

_____

_____

_____

_____

_____

_____

_____

_____

_____

_____

_____

_____

_____

_____

Prayer:

_____

Grateful gift:

_____

DAY 5

BEFORE YOU READ ANOTHER WORD, LISTEN TO the song "*Mountain of God*" by the band Third Day. I urge you to write the words down. The journey is long, there is always a mountain to climb, and God will be there with you on the mountaintop.

Talk about a goal that was your hardest to reach. What was your uphill battle? How did you keep climbing and what was the outcome? What did it teach you about BEing goal-minded?

_____

_____

_____

_____

_____

_____

_____

_____

_____

_____

Prayer:

_____

Grateful gift:

_____

Week 3

BE Prepared

"By failing to prepare, you are preparing to fail."
Benjamin Franklin

2.4....112....26.2 – I Am An *Iron Woman*

I LOVE TO SWIM, BIKE, AND RUN. TRIATHLONS
have played a huge role for Sean and me, especially before
children. Living in Central Florida the first years of our
marriage afforded us the opportunity to swim in pristine
lakes, run among lush citrus groves on deserted dirt, and
bike some of the highest elevation in Florida—a whopping
345 feet.

Triathlons taught me about being prepared and taught
me about prayer. Not only how to train for a 2.4-mile swim,
a 112-mile bike ride and a marathon run (26.2 miles), but
how to change a flat bike tire, how to eat, and how to
encourage other competitors. I was an overweight child
growing up in Kentucky on fried children, RC®, and bis-
cuits. My breakfast included an Ale-8® and a Zinger®. At
that point, the only main sports for girls were cheerleading
and tennis—neither of which I was skilled. I began swimming, running, and biking in college largely through the
encouragement of great gal pals. So, when Sean said, "let's

do a triathlon," my competitive spirit jumped in. To me, everything about triathlon is fun and rewarding. People of all skills and ages cheer you to the finish line. You write your age in black sharpie on your calf. How fun is that? I completed my first triathlon in October, 1996 behind several women ages 65 and older. We participated in all distances of triathlons for over fifteen years. The pinnacle was training and competing in the 1999 Iron Man Lake Placid, the first US continental Iron Man competition.

Preparation is 100 percent perspiration and requires discipline and dedication. We trained close to 500 hours in seven months. It was worth every minute because we finished. The Scripture below was written on my mirror, in my car, on my bike, on t-shirts, and on a card in the bag I took to every race.

God will always give us the strength for what He has planned for us.

"I can do everything through God who gives me strength." Philippians 4:13

DAY 1

*"Give me six hours to chop down a tree and I will spend
the first four sharpening the axe." Abraham Lincoln*

DURING THE LONG BIKE TRAINING, MY FRIEND
Kim was my inspiration. We had a game to pass the five-to
seven-hour bike rides. We called it the 'alpha prayer'. We
started at A and with every letter to Z, we said a prayer
for something or someone that began with that letter.
Sometimes we would even sing it as we repeated the
alphabet again and again. And God heard every prayer.

Look at your calendar and think about upcoming
events, projects and goals. Who is your "Kim"? Do you
need a project map? Who needs to help you? What do you
need for success? Organization? Time?

_____

_____

_____

_____

_____

Prayer:

_____

Grateful gift:

_____

Day 2

"However, as it is written: 'What no eye has seen, what no ear has heard, and what no human mind has conceived' the things God has prepared for those who love him." 1 Corinthians 2:9

DESCRIBE A PROJECT, EVENT, RACE, PRESENTAtion, or something that required you to be completely prepared. What was it? How long did it take? Who was your support team? What was the outcome? What tools did you pull from the toolbox to be fully prepared? What did you learn? What typically keeps you from being prepared?

_____

_____

_____

_____

_____

_____

_____

_____

Prayer:

_____

Grateful gift:

_____

Day 3

"Be prepared, and prepare yourself, you and all your companies that are assembled about you and be a guard for them." Ezekiel 38:7

UNLIKE YESTERDAY, WHERE I HOPE YOU FELT joy and accomplishment, today, might be painful. Describe a project, event, or something when you did not prepare What stopped you from being focused? What tools didn't you use? Why not? Who could have been part of your company to help you prepare?

_____

_____

_____

_____

_____

_____

_____

_____

_____

Prayer:

_____

Grateful gift:

_____

Day 4

"So, you, too, must keep watch! For you don't know what day your Lord is coming." Matthew 24:42

THE ASPIRIN STORY AT THE BEGINNING OF THE book ended with a reminder that we do not know how long we will live.

My "spell" at the baseball game was a reminder that I need to BE prepared and live a life worthy of the God who created me.

Have you had a near-death experience or epiphany encouraging you to BE your BEst self? Describe how the last few months have inspired you.

_____

_____

_____

_____

_____

_____

_____

_____

Prayer:

_____

Grateful gift:

_____

Day 5

"Keep awake therefore, because you do not know the day or the hour." Matthew 25:13

READ MATTHEW 25:1-13 AND WRITE DOWN some thoughts about the five foolish and five wise brides-maids. Five of them did not take oil for their lamps. The other five took flasks of oil as they waited for the bridegroom.

Camping and hiking are two of my favorite activities. I love the preparation, the outdoors, and experiencing God's beauty in a simple setting. You need a map, compass, water, supplies, tent, backpack, and the right shoes. My Uncle Billy was an adventurer and visited all the world's wonders. My blessing was the two weeks he and I rafted and hiked the Grand Canyon. We spent months preparing and with one exception: I nailed it. I forgot a mirror and tweezers. While my eyebrows were quite a site upon returning to civilization, it was a great reminder of what we can live with—and without.

The best way to make God laugh is to tell Him our plans. It is one thing to plan and another to BE prepared. How are you prepared to BEst serve God?

_____

_____

_____

_____

BE 12

Prayer:

_____

Grateful gift:

_____

Week 4

REINVENT YOURSELF

Make every effort to add to your faith, goodness; and to goodness, knowledge; and to knowledge, self-control; and to self-control, perseverance; and to perseverance, godliness; and to godliness, mutual affection; and to mutual affection, love. Therefore, my brothers and sisters, make every effort to confirm your calling and election. For if you do these things, you will never stumble and you will receive a rich welcome into the eternal kingdom of our Lord and Savior Jesus. 2 Peter 1:5-7, 10-11

THE SEASONS WE EXPERIENCE MAY BE VIBRANT like the fall leaves, cold and dreary, bright and cheery, or perhaps warm and sunny. The good and bad news is that seasons come and go. At some point, you may encounter a season of reinvention. A snow storm may have forced you into this season or you may have decided that you needed a new, BEtter you.

As I rose strong from the "lost year" armed with lessons and growth, I found a new attitude and approach to life. The Sea Star, more commonly known as the starfish, became my symbol. These beautiful marine animals usually have five legs and can be colorful and are seen in over 400 shapes and sizes. They are the only creature that when they lose a limb, they grow a new one.

Growing a new limb is incredibly helpful when a predator injures you. Guess how long it takes them to regenerate a new limb? About one year. Yet, that is about how long it took me to reinvent myself after a series of "predators" took my arm. Let me be clear: I allowed the predators to attack me because I didn't stand for my BEliefs and I didn't BElieve in myself.

Day 1

Read the verses above from 2 Peter. Describe what these verses mean to you and the season you are in right now. Just like the 12 Steps to Recovery tell us, I first had to admit I needed to reinvent. And I needed to rebuild my village so others could help me. It started small with my most valuable ally and partner, my husband. Then I began reconnecting with people I valued and many of whom I had lost touch. Women fall and we get back up stronger than before.

How are you living your calling? What areas do you need reinvention? Name the people in your village who will help.

_____

_____

_____

_____

_____

_____

_____

_____

_____

_____

_____

_____

Day 2

Who are the predators that devise "taking your leg"? Are they the demons in your mind that tell you can't or you're not smart enough? Are they family or coworkers or complete strangers that make you feel less significant? God made you and God loves you. Identify what is holding you back and reflect on your values. Do you need more faith, goodness, knowledge, or self-control today?

_____

_____

_____

_____

_____

_____

_____

_____

_____

_____

_____

_____

_____

_____

_____

_____

Day 3

"Jabez cried out to the God of Israel, 'Oh, that you would bless me and enlarge my territory! Let your hand be with me and keep me from harm so that I will be free from pain.' And God granted his request."
1 Chronicles 4:9-10

My dear friend and sister in Christ, Jules, is a sage member of my village. As I confided in her during my lost year, she shared with me how she had cried the prayer of Jabez for thirty days and how it helped her emerge from a dark place.

Explain the areas of your life where you need God to bless you. Describe what enlarging your territory and keeping you from harm means to your situation. What 'possibilities' are you seeking?

Bless me with the tools I need to achieve my calling. You can start today by thanking God for your blessings. Now, how does your territory need enlarging?

_____

_____

_____

_____

_____

_____

_____

_____

Day 4

My lost year that I have described included working for an organization that did not fit me or my skills. Whether we think we can change the world, or we think the grass is greener, we make mistakes. After months of prayer and counsel, I made a change. It was the scariest step I have ever taken. I had failed, and I needed to figure it out. I immersed myself in God's Word and countless self-development books.

One great read was *Make Your Bed,* by Admiral William McRaven. The Admiral's premise is that accomplishing a task first thing in the morning sets you on the right path for the entire day. Small steps may yield great accomplishments. Keep moving onward as you look up for God to guide you.

After coming off a year of defeat, I had to accomplish some small tasks. First, I love to swim, but for years had been going through the motions of swimming for an hour at least three times a week. Yet, I wasn't getting better. My daughters equated my stroke to a chicken wing and my flip-turn looked like I was drowning. I needed a village, so I joined the St. Pete Masters swim group and learned how to flip-turn. I now swim with experts who push me, correct my stroke, and while some of them may still laugh at my flip-turn, they encourage me.

Describe small tasks that will help straighten your path.

_____

_____

_____

Day 5

Value Assessment Day

Today is your day of reflection. Look back on your notes. What was the most "BE moment" of this past month? What did you learn about BEing a hard worker, goal-minded, and prepared? What cape will you wear?

_____

_____

_____

_____

_____

_____

_____

_____

_____

_____

_____

_____

_____

_____

_____

_____

_____

_____

BE ENCOURAGING

Do Ordinary Things With Extraordinary Love

BE Encouraging

"But encourage one another daily as long as it is called Today, so that no one may be hardened by sin's deceitfulness." Hebrews 3:13

My grandfather always said, "You catch more flies with honey than with vinegar." He used this saying to remind me that we are called to encourage others whenever we can. My calling to write this book stemmed from wanting to have a larger conversation about honey, not vinegar. Each day we have an opportunity to be extraordinary with our words and deeds.

Encouragement gives hope and hope can change a person's life. Look at the origin of the word "encourage," which is the Old French word *encoragier*, meaning "make strong, hearten."

We give courage and strength to others with words and deeds. Whether cheering on a kid from the sidelines, using positive words to praise a family member or giving a friend a genuine compliment, make someone stronger and BEtter.

Read Luke 10:25-37 and the story of the Good Samaritan. I was disturbed hearing this as a child. How could any one pass by someone that was hurt? Yet, I do it every day. How often are we too caught up in ourselves to notice those around us that need healing? Describe when you have been a Good Samaritan.

_____

_____

_____

There are moments to show encouragement every day. Seize them for you never know when you may have saved a life. Recently, when flying on a Southwest flight, I was reading the Bible and journaling. I noticed a young male flight attendant continued to walk by and glance at my reading. Once given clearance to walk about, I sauntered to the galley and began a simple conversation. He opened up about his life, how he landed his job, and his struggles. He was in great pain. I gave him several ideas of books to read, and we had a God-filled conversation.

Prior to landing, when he was collecting the final items from passengers, he slipped me a note. He shared how timely and pertinent the encouragement I provided and how thankful he was that God put me there on that day. He shared his plans of how he was going to serve God.

What appeared to be ordinary made someone feel extraordinary. Opportunities abound to lift up others and, in the process, I am confident that you too will rise high.

BE thoughtful, kind, and compassionate.

BE THOUGHTFUL

"From everyone who had been given much, much
will be demanded; and from the one who has been
entrusted with much, much more will be asked."
Luke 12:48

THOUGHTFUL PEOPLE HAVE A STRONG VALUE system. They listen, are open-minded, they recognize people, and are considerate of others' feelings. In our rush to get it done, we forget the simple act of thoughtfulness. Much to my daughters' chagrin, I write uplifting quotes and Bible verses in lipstick on mirrors, on post-it notes, in their backpacks and under their pillows. I put motivational quotes in the swim locker room, on the walls, and beside the dinner plates. I want them to know it's the little things that count. While their successes in school and in sports is important, following the Golden Rule of loving God and others is paramount.

Think of thoughtful moments you see during the day. I was raised in the South and everyone acknowledges other drivers. My father waved to everyone. Southern protocol is when another driver lets you in front of them, you give a little wave. When my oldest daughter Megan started to drive her sister Molly to school, the wave was Molly's job.

She was to wave to people that let them merge in traffic or let them go in front of them. Try it with a smile on your face and see what comes back to you.

Simply put, thoughtfulness is considering the needs of other people. The energy you need to BE thoughtful includes opening your eyes to those around you. This week, I hope you will put down your phone, limit social media, stop binge Netflix watching, and BE aware of the needs of others.

Day 1

"Therefore encourage one another and build each other
up, just as in fact you are doing." 1 Thessalonians 5:11

TODAY IS YOUR CHANCE. LOOK AROUND YOU
and find at least three people who need encouragement.
Maybe it is an email, a call, or lifting up the service worker
collecting your trash or the server at the restaurant. Describe
what you did and the outcome.

_____

_____

_____

_____

_____

_____

_____

_____

_____

Prayer:

_____

Grateful gift:

_____

Day 2

"Then the Lord said to him, 'Take off your sandals, for the place where you are standing is holy ground."Acts 7:33

MY DAUGHTER MOLLY ATTENDS A CHRISTIAN summer camp for young women. Merri-Mac is sacred ground to me and each time I step foot on the property in North Carolina, I am filled with God's spirit.

Do you have a holy place? If so, where is it?

The camp continues to develop her into a faith-filled, loving young lady. One of their activities is what I call "rid the rock." The girls write a word on a rock that another has negatively used to describe them. It may have been to their face or rumors they heard. They take that rock and hurl it far into the lake. They also write what someone has said to describe their beautiful traits. They keep that rock to be reminded the power of words can build up or tear down someone.

Today, find a rock or something that can be plunged far away and never found. Write the suffocating negative that someone said to you or about you. I know your pain recalling the words. People have told me I was fat, untrustworthy, selfish, that I "couldn't handle the job", and more. I threw all those lies deep in the Gulf of Mexico because I am God's child and His perfect creation. Pray for those people who were unkind. They need God's love. Describe people who encourage you and how they have helped you BE BEtter.

_____

_____

_____

_____

_____

_____

_____

_____

_____

_____

_____

_____

_____

_____

_____

Prayer:

_____

Grateful gift:

_____

Day 3

"Gentle words bring life and health; a deceitful tongue stirs wrath." Proverbs 18:4

How many times have you opened your mouth only to say something hurtful or deceitful?

My mouth stirs wrath more times than I would like to recall. To bridle my tongue, I began to focus on pre-conversations. What interactions was I going to have, with whom, and what outcome did I desire? I want to encourage, not tear down.

Think of your interactions today, and describe what you will do to make them more positive and encouraging.

_____

_____

_____

_____

_____

_____

_____

_____

Prayer

_____

Grateful Gift:

_____

Day 4

Congratulations. You're the perfect you. Just the person the world needs to fill your shoes and do your job. Share your incredible 'you-ness' with everyone lucky enough to know you.

MY SECOND MOM, MIGNON, WHO WAS A KEY part of the village that raised me, sent me the above message when I was in college. Mignon's eyes were always opened to other's needs. These words have encouraged me for the last 30 years.

I love colors and crazy pants. The other day, while running, I saw a women in a bright, happy pair of running pants. I stopped, which is always a bad sign because I may not start again and told her she looked great in them. Her reply warmed my heart. "Thank you honey, I have lost twenty-five pounds to fit in these; you've made my day."

Write down twenty encouraging words and think about how you will use them today. Think of a time that you received an encouraging word of support. How did it make you feel?

_____

_____

_____

_____

_____

_____

_____

_____

_____

_____

_____

_____

_____

Prayer

_____

Grateful Gift:

_____

Day 5

*"Therefore, we do not lose heart. Though outwardly
we are wasting away, yet inwardly we are being
renewed day by day." 2 Corinthians 4:16*

BEHIND EVERY SUCCESSFUL WOMAN IS
someone who built her up with encouragement. Name
women who have encouraged you. Write them a note of
thanks and appreciation. In addition, describe at least five
people that you have built up. What made you take the time
to encourage them?

_____

_____

_____

_____

_____

_____

_____

_____

_____

Prayer:

_____

Grateful gift:

_____

Week 2

BE Kind

"Everyone should be quick to listen, slow to speak and slow to become angry." James 1:19

CHARLES DUHIGG'S, *THE POWER OF HABIT,* presents brilliant lessons on BEcoming your best self. He describes the difference in who you are and who you want to be is ***what*** you are doing. His cue, routing, reward theory on habits calls for changing your routine to receive the rewards you desire. About forty percent of what you do happens on autopilot. Habits are your brain's way of saving energy. The cue triggers the habit, you engage in the routine and you receive a reward for completing the routine.

You can change your habits by changing your routine. Kindness has the power to change the world. The times I regret the most are the ones where I did not show kindness and the moments when I could have been more inclusive, taken the high road, shut my mouth, and when I could have been the light under the lamp.

Mark 12:30-31 proclaims the greatest commandments. To abide by these means to put others before ourselves. Write down the commandments, memorize these verses, and commit to living them. You, sweet sister, can change the world, one action at a time. As you think about what the Word says in Mark 12:30-31, describe your habits as they relate to loving God, yourself and others.

Day 1

"What causes fights and quarrels among you? Don't they come from your desires that battle within you? You desire but do not have, so you kill. You covet but you cannot get what you want, so you quarrel and fight. You do not have because you do not ask God. When you ask, you do not receive, because you ask with wrong motives, that you may spend what you get on your pleasures." James 4:1-3

ON TOO MANY OCCASIONS, MY "OLD SELF" stirred strife because I wanted something someone else had, and I felt I deserved it. God's grace has led me to a place of content. Describe a time you initiated conflict because you weren't happy with yourself or your situation. Evaluate your motives. Take this time to remember your feelings and list a few of your grateful items to remind yourself of your blessings. What is stopping you from BEing kind?

_____

_____

_____

_____

Prayer:

_____

Grateful gift:

_____

Day 2

"Judge not, that ye be not judged." Matthew 7:1-5

YOU CANNOT JUDGE AND BE KIND AT THE SAME
time. Women can be cruel. We look around us—and often
out of insecurity—about our bodies, our jobs, our children,
our finances, we say zingers, words that sting.

Speaking of zingers, the yellow plastic icing coated cakes,
I had them for breakfast with an Ale-8® in middle and most
of high school. That is important for this week because I
was a fat kid with unhealthy eating habits. My insecurities
caused me to make fun of cheerleaders and others who had
talents that I did not. What words and actions are "judgy"
and prevent you from BEing kind?

_____

_____

_____

_____

_____

_____

_____

Prayer:

_____

Grateful Gift:

_____

Day 3

"A word aptly spoken is like apples of gold in settings of silver." Proverbs 25:11

WHAT ARE SOME WAYS THAT YOU CAN MAKE sure you rise above the crowd when they are doing or saying what you know is wrong? BE aware of negative words coming from other people. How do you react?

_____

_____

_____

_____

_____

_____

_____

_____

_____

_____

Prayer:

_____

Grateful gift:

_____

Day 4

"Not only so, but we also glory in our sufferings, because we know that suffering produces perseverance; perseverance, character; and character, hope." Romans 5:3-4

A SIGN OF TRUE CHARACTER IS HOW YOU TREAT those who can do nothing for you. With kindness as your value, you understand that people are in all walks of life. Some may be suffering and need hope. A true test of character is not how you are on your best days, but how you act on your worst days. Author Matthew Kelley in his book, *Perfectly Yourself*, describes doing the next right thing. Think about your character. Describe why and how you treated someone with kindness. Be specific as you detail your motives and how you did the next right thing. Describe a time when you were at your worst and how you reacted. Did you do the next right thing? How can you do the next right thing to BE kind?

_____

_____

_____

_____

_____

_____

_____

_____

Prayer:

_____

Grateful Gift:

_____

Day 5

"So, in everything, do to others what you would have them do to you." Matthew 7:12

TODAY IS YOUR RANDOM ACTS OF KINDNESS day. List at least three things you can do today and for whom. You can leave a five dollar bill where someone will find it, give food and a drink to the people that pick up your trash, write a note to a friend you haven't seen in a while. Describe how you felt when you offered kindness and expected nothing in return.

_____

_____

_____

_____

_____

_____

_____

_____

Prayer:

_____

Grateful Gift:

_____

Week 3

BE Compassionate

"Praise be to the God and Father of our Lord Jesus Christ, the Father of compassion and the God of all comfort, who comforts us in all our troubles, so that we can comfort those in any trouble." 2 Corinthians 1:3-4

"If you want others to be happy, practice compassion. If you want to be happy, practice compassion." Dalai Lama

THE DALAI LAMA MAKES IT SOUND FAIRLY easy. Happiness equals compassion. Compassion equals happiness. We all strive to be happy, so let's BE compassionate. The most compassionate people I know have similar qualities. They act on their empathy. They are kind to themselves. They are mindful and present.

Compassion and empathy are not my strongest strengths. One of the best development assessments I have taken is *StrengthsFinders 2.0*, by Thomas Rath. Before reading the book, you take a quiz to determine your top strengths. The premise is to maximize your strengths instead of fixing your weaknesses. The book describes your strengths in detail and how to best interact with others. I strongly encourage you to consider this assessment and book. It has helped me BE a BEtter leader, wife, mom and friend

I consider myself a kind person so I had to dig deep into empathy and compassion, and they are not the same. Empathy or altruism is our ability to take the perspective and feel the emotions of others. My wonderful husband Sean is good at this. I am sort of "put on your big girl panties and boots and let's roll." The joke in our house is, "if the bone isn't protruding or blood gushing, don't ask Mama for help." Compassion, on the other hand, is showing concern and desire to help those in need through actions, words and deeds. I spend a lot of time on this value.

Day 1

Some men took a man who was not able to move his body to Jesus. He was carried on a bed. They looked for a way to take the man into the house where Jesus was. But they could not find a way to take him in because of so many people. They made a hole in the roof over where Jesus stood. Then they let the bed with the sick man on it down before Jesus. Luke 5:17-19

I PICTURE THIS STORY EVERY TIME I READ THIS Scripture. It causes me pause as I reflect on the friendship of these men. They were not going to take *no* for an answer. They were going to put their sick friend before Jesus. Describe when a friend has gone above and beyond for you. How did it change your attitude about compassion? Describe a situation when you have 'carried' a friend. What were your sacrifices and how did this bring you joy?

_____

_____

_____

_____

Prayer:

_____

Grateful Gift:

_____

Day 2

Therefore, as God's chosen people, holy and dearly loved, clothe yourselves with compassion, kindness, humility, gentleness and patience. Bear with each other and forgive one another if any of you has a grievance against someone. Forgive as the Lord forgave you. And over all these virtues put on love, which binds them all together in perfect unity. Colossians 3:12-17

THIS BEAUTIFUL SCRIPTURE LISTS MANY values. I urge you to write this down somewhere where you see it every day. Describe in detail what the following words mean to you and how you display each of these values.

Compassion: _____

_____

Kindness: _____

_____

Humility: _____

_____

Gentleness: _____

_____

Patience: _____

_____

Forgiveness: _____

_____

Prayer:

_____

Grateful Gift:

_____

Day 3

"Be kind and compassionate to one another forgiving each other." Ephesians 4:32

TRAITS OF TRULY COMPASSIONATE PEOPLE include being mindful, having high emotional intelligence, and expressing gratitude. And they are kind. Check that box; last week we learned to BE more kind. This concept of emotional intelligence is becoming more relevant. People with high emotional intelligence are in control of their emotions, clearly express their emotions, handle interpersonal relationships judiciously, and benefit from criticism. How can you improve your emotional intelligence in order to BE more compassionate?

_____

_____

_____

_____

_____

_____

_____

Prayer:

_____

Grateful Gift:

_____

DAY 4

*Judge not, and you will not be judged; condemn not,
and you will not be condemned; forgive, and you will
be forgiven; give, and it will be given to you. Good
measure, pressed down, shaken together, running over,
will be put into your lap. For with the measure you
use it will be measured back to you. Luke 6:37-38*

YOU KNOW I STRUGGLE WITH BEING COMPAS-
sionate. I know one way I can grow in this value is to stop
judging others and start producing good measure. I have
a problem managing my expectations and this personality
trait interferes with my ability to show compassion. Have
you experienced similar situations as described below?

- "I sent her a great gift for her birthday and she was too
  busy to even call me."
- "She didn't even say thank you for the time and energy
  I spent to help her."
- "He knew this was a tough day for me and didn't even
  ask about it."

Read this again: "for with the measure you use it will
measured back to you." Put love, kindness, encouragement,
and compassion is a big blender. Keep adding more, even
when you think you can't. Turn it on and let it overflow.
For it is in giving that we receive. Managing expectations
requires you to let go and let God. What is holding you
back from BEing thoughtful, kind, and compassionate?

_____

_____

_____

_____

_____

_____

_____

_____

_____

_____

_____

_____

_____

_____

Prayer:

_____

_____

Grateful Gift:

_____

_____

Day 5

*"But to you who are listening I say: Love your enemies,
do good to those who hate you, bless those who curse
you, pray for those who mistreat you." Luke 6:27-28*

*"Do not repay evil with evil or insult with insult. On
the contrary repay evil with blessing, because to this
you were called so that you may inherit a blessing."
1 Peter 3:9*

THESE TWO VERSES GIVE US GUIDELINES FOR
showing compassion to others. How can we love our enemies? How can we not throw back a jab at someone who
has insulted us? God tells us we must love our enemies and
bless them.

I have been hurt by people and I have hurt people with
my actions and deeds. We can commit today to loving and
blessing at least one enemy. As I was writing this book, I
opened old wounds. I consulted with those wiser than me,
and I prayed for how I could bless this person when I felt
such anger. For forty days, I wrote the name on a card and
prayed at least three times. On the fortieth day, I landed on
my knees and asked God to bless them and their family. The
freedom I felt was like I was flying on eagle's wings. From that
day forward, I rarely have a thought of that person except in
prayer. Describe an 'enemy'. How have you blessed those
who cursed you? What is your prayer for them?

_____

_____

_____

_____

_____

_____

_____

_____

_____

_____

_____

_____

_____

_____

_____

_____

_____

_____

_____

_____

Prayer:

_____

Grateful Gift:

_____

Week 4

Re Energize Those
Around You

Open your Bible and read the book of Ruth in the Old Testament. Ruth was one of the strongest female characters in the Old Testament. Ruth's story is one of loyalty, love, and perseverance.

In short: Naomi is Ruth's mother-in-law. Naomi's husband dies. Ten years later, Naomi's son, Ruth's husband, also dies. Naomi, Ruth, and her sister Orpah were left in a land without husbands, which in those days was a dire situation for women. Naomi plead with the two young women to leave her and go to a new land and reestablish themselves. Ruth stayed.

Throughout the various trials of Ruth and Naomi, they support and watch out for each other. In the end, Naomi plays matchmaker and connects Ruth with a righteous man, Boaz, that provides for both of them. The love stories in Ruth are powerful and the amazing part is Ruth becomes the great-grandmother of Israel's heroic king David.

I identify with this story in many ways. The two Ruth's in my life taught me values of loyalty and family. My mother-in-law, Ruth, was a beacon of love spreading kindness to everyone she touched. She never had a harsh word to say about anyone and put family above all. My other Ruth, whom I am named after, is my aunt. She is the definition of loyalty and friendship. One example is her gang's monthly bridge game. Aunt Ruth and her gal pals have been playing bridge the third Tuesday of every month for over thirty years. They never let soccer games, work, or fixing dinner get in the way of their time together. As a child, I would often sit on the stairs when she hosted them and just listen. They talked about work, laughed, recipes, and encouraged each other with whatever they were working on. Aunt Ruth has a village. They have lost children, husbands, and jobs. They have celebrated weddings and shared countless joys. They energize each other. These ladies taught me about friendship. They weren't obsessed with talking about their children, and they never said a harsh or judging word about someone else.

You may have traditions with friends. If you do, value them. If you don't, consider planning some. The busy trap is a snare that keeps you from joy. My gal pal groups gather regularly in various ways. It is hard to make the time and commitment and when I have faltered from our time together, I feel lost. My village is full of brave, caring women who are centered and I need them. I BElieve the impact of purposeful gathering among friends is critical to long lasting relationships.

Day 1

"Many are the plans in a person's heart, but it is the Lord's purpose that prevails." Proverbs 19:21

No matter how long you have been driving, the blind spots still catch you. Blind spots cause accidents. Identify your blind spot. Are you loyal and relational? What areas need a little extra looking over your shoulder? This month we BEcame more encouraging, thoughtful, kind, and compassionate. Which of these values needed your attention the most? Why?

_____

_____

_____

_____

_____

_____

_____

_____

_____

_____

_____

_____

_____

_____

Day 2

"But I tell you, love your enemies and pray for those who persecute you." Matthew 5:44

DO YOU HAVE AN ENEMY THAT NEEDS YOUR encouragement or kindness? "Enemy" may be a harsh word, but you know what it looks like. It's the mom at school that can never have a kind word about your child. It's the co-worker who talks about your flaws to everyone in the office and your boss. I urge you to stop now and write a prayer for them. They are probably not thinking about you near as much as you are them. Pray for them, and you will be lifted of the negative burden and doubt that is clouding your thoughts.

Day 3

THE BIBLICAL RUTH, MY MOTHER-IN-LAW, AND
my Aunt Ruth shared a common value: loyalty. Describe a
tradition of loyalty you have *or* one you would like to start.
If it is one you have, reflect on it now. What has this tradition meant to you? If you would like to start one, what does
it take? Who will be in this group or activity you want to
start? How will you proceed to get it going?

_____

_____

_____

_____

_____

_____

_____

_____

_____

_____

_____

_____

_____

_____

_____

Day 4

"For we are God's handiwork, created in Christ Jesus to do good works, which God prepared in advance for us to do." Ephesians 2:10

FOR YOU GAL PALS THAT ARE AS OLD AS ME, YOU may remember the flag or monogrammed needlepoint belts. I loved them and my best friend could create one in weeks. I tried just like I tried to make that skirt in Home Ec. My handiwork needs work. I am humbled when I think of how God created me to do good work.

What good work have you BEen doing to develop your values? How did you show kindness, compassion and encouragement to someone today?

_____

_____

_____

_____

_____

_____

_____

_____

_____

_____

_____

Day 5

Read Romans 12:9-21. Explain what makes love sincere.

_____

_____

_____

What evil do you hate?

_____

_____

_____

To whom are you devoted?

_____

_____

_____

Describe a time when you have been joyful in hope, patient in affliction, and faithful in prayer.

_____

_____

_____

Describe a time when you felt like revenge was the best solution. What lessons did you learn and how does this Scripture make you rethink what it means to be at peace with everyone?

_____

_____

Have you fed an enemy? Not with poison, but with love and good.

BE FAITHFUL

I Try To Win This War...

BE Faithful

"Faith is being certain of what we hope for and confident in what we do not see." Hebrews 11:1

TAKE A MINUTE BEFORE WE START TODAY TO listen to Lauren Daigle's song, *"Trust In You."* Write down the chorus or what words resonate with you. I have learned that God's timing is not mine and that it is perfect. While He may not move the mountains or part the waters I want, I have learned that when I put all my trust in Him, I am never disappointed.

My faith has been tested and strengthened. My mother-in-law Ruth was kind, considerate, funny, and never had a harsh word to say about anyone. She was supportive and always present. She was tough and beat breast cancer in the early 1990s. On Thanksgiving Day 2008, Sean and I received a call from Sean's step-father Bob that his mother Ruth was ill. She had been sick for several months with stomach issues. If you haven't realized the saint my husband is, you are about to hear of his incredible character. We lived in Florida and his mom in Kentucky. Her diagnosis was a rare stomach cancer. A few months and many doctors' appointments later, Sean and I had few answers. No matter the joys or defeats, Sean and I are one. We make big decisions together after prayer and thoughtful communication.

We decided that Sean would leave his job to care for his mother. As it happened, we did not know how long he would need to commute back and forth. He spent most of the next six months in Kentucky. I had no idea how we would afford our home, food, his travel to Kentucky, and our kids' school. I was running my own company. I was scared. I recall standing at the check-out line in Publix running the debit card and praying there was money in the account.

My survival team was God's hands and my small village of four gal pals that carried me on their backs. Beth, Kim, Katja, and Tiffany laughed and cried with me. They were always there to give some piece of wisdom. Sean was a saint, making sure he interpreted all the tests and physician comments and making sure his mom had all she needed. Ruth's health continued to decline but her spirit never wavered. She was joyful until the end. The day she decided to end treatment, she smiled as we talked about Megan, Molly, and her amazing legacy. I was mad that God took her from me and that our daughters wouldn't know this remarkable woman. A few months after she died, I sat at her graveside just like I had Mignon's years earlier. The only words that I kept hearing was, "live their legacy." Both Ruth and Mignon were servants, peaceful and patient. How was I going to BE any of those when I felt betrayed by God? I needed to BE a servant, to find peace and to BE patient as I trusted God.

Sisters, the pain of someone you love so dearly being taken from you can be debilitating. I pray you have your tools to heal and move forward. Friends, therapy, trusting

God's plan, and honoring your loved ones' legacy may help. Let me share some ways we have coped. On the anniversary of Ruth, Mignon, Billy, Ken and Daddy, we celebrate their life by watching a sunset, eating their favorite meal, and spend the evening talking about them. I also write a letter to each of them on their birthdays. God's timing is perfect, even when it is painful.

BE a servant, peaceful and patient.

Week 1

Be a Servant

"Never lacking in zeal, but keep your spiritual fervor, serving the Lord." Romans 12:11

I WROTE MY FIRST PURPOSE STATEMENT WHEN I was twenty-nine years old. I was newly married and we had just moved to Orlando. I didn't have a job. I didn't know anyone and was unsure of my next chapter. God delivered two women that remain my dearest friends, supporters, confidantes, and gals who taught me about purpose and service. Twenty years later, Beth and Kim still serve as my accountability partners. They keep me grounded in faith, are honest with me about my blind spots, and bring out the best in me. Good friends not only serve you but are willing to be served. Our trio read the, *On Purpose Person,* by Kevin McCarthy and, *The Path,* by Laurie Beth Jones. Both books are excellent references for personal mission creation and action. We wrote our mission statements and held each other accountable. I refer to my statement often and refresh it every few years. Service is part of my purpose. Romans 12:11 reminds me to use my energy to serve the Lord. I found my best tool for living the service value was an armor. The full armor of God described in Ephesians 6.

I have always been fascinated with knights that wore bright, shiny armor and defended their cause. They were usually portrayed as heroic, valiant, unbeatable, and loyal. They fought until death for their cause. Read Ephesians 6:10-20. Paul describes weapons that we need to be fully armed not only to fight the enemy but to serve. The seven weapons of our armor are:

- The Belt of Truth
- The Breastplate of Righteousness
- The Shoes of Peace
- The Shield of Faith
- The Helmet of Salvation
- The Sword of the Spirit
- Prayer

Day 1

"Stand firm then, with the belt of truth buckled around your waist." Ephesians 6:14

I LOVE BELTS AND THE BOLDER THE BUCKLE, the brighter the bling, the better. I *could* wear them to hold up my pants, but mainly I do it for appearance. Without a belt, everything would be loose and scattered. Belts help us stand up tall because we aren't fidgeting to keep our pants up. The Bible commonly refers to a girdle as a belt. A girdle, when I was growing up, was what my grandmother wore under her Sunday dress to keep everything in place. Today, it is our beloved Spanx®, which also increases our confidence and keeps the bum in place.

A few weeks ago, we jumped right in to BEing honest. So today, as we think of how the belt of truth keeps it all together, ask yourself: how are you the one who shares the truth? How are you spreading the truth of God's love? It might be at the dinner table talking to your seventeen-year-old or being a role model of kindness. Maybe it is not engaging in harmful conversation or replying to a social media post that angers you. Describe how the belt of truth fits you.

_____

_____

_____

_____

_____

Prayer:

_____

Grateful Gift:

_____

Day 2

"with the breastplate of righteousness in place."
Ephesians 6:14b

IN ANCIENT ROMAN DAYS, THE BREASTPLATE of a suit of armor could weigh seventy pounds. I often feel like I am carrying a heavy load—whether it is another's burden, maybe a problem among friends or at work. My heart is heavy and it hurts.

Yet, the BE 12 energy we are absorbing, combined with our breastplate, protects our heart. Righteousness means justice, which literally translated is the quality of BEing upright. Just like the breastplate that stops the arrow from piercing your heart, how do your values protect your heart? Describe how you guard your heart to BE standing tall as you fulfill your relationship with God and others.

Prayer:

Grateful Gift:

Day 3

"and with your feet fitted with the readiness that comes from the gospel of peace." Ephesians 6:15

EVIL STIRS UP WARS OF DISTURBANCE AND unrest. You lose your balance when there is division. The use of "balance" is common among many women's conversation as we seek to BE our BEst at home, work, and play.

I went on a quest to find a better word for "balance" and I came up with *center*. When I am centered, I am at peace.

Being centered is the place of equilibrium where your values and actions meet. Your center may look different on a Saturday with your family versus a Tuesday working on a large project. Imagine riding a bike. You need to be centered to get the best speed and not fall to one side or the other. Our family does a Sunday calendar review. This has proven to be a great tool for making sure our values are reflected in our time and talents. Sean and I are then able to make work accommodations so we are centering on what is most important, our family. Describe how you are centered with your feet firmly planted. What tricks do you use to stay centered?

_____

_____

_____

_____

_____

_____

Prayer:

_____

Grateful Gift:

_____

DAY 4

*..take up the shield of faith, with which you can
extinguish all the flaming arrows of the evil one.
Ephesians 6:16*

FAITH CAN EXTINGUISH EVIL! OUR FAITH IS
tested in many ways. Death, sickness, financial challenges,
and betrayal are some arrows aimed to pierce our heart.
Describe your shield of faith. How do you hold the shield
high? Is it with prayer, scripture, Bible study? What arrows
are flying your way today?

_____

_____

_____

_____

_____

_____

Prayer:

_____

Grateful Gift:

_____

Day 5

*"take the helmet of salvation and the sword of the
Spirit, which is the word of God." Ephesians 6:17*

MY CAREER IN HEALTHCARE AFFORDED ME THE
opportunity to be engaged in countless helmet discussions.
The helmet laws can be contentious, but I believe the one
fact we can agree is that helmets protect our brains. The
brain is the most complex organ in humans and controls
the nervous system. While we know our heart keeps us alive,
our brain keeps us functioning.

The study of brain health is one of the fastest areas of
research. Many of us are worried that we may suffer from
Alzheimer's or other diseases of the brain. We are eating
more blueberries and playing brain games. Think hard and
be deliberate as you answer today's questions. What are
you doing to renew and protect your mind? Arrows fly our
way every day. We are consumed with information through
social media and we are challenged to decipher the truth
from fiction. How are you challenging the status quo and
focusing on your values? What values do you use to renew
your salvation? The sword Paul describes in Ephesians 6:17
is the Bible. I challenge you today to write down, memorize
and live scripture that renews you.

_____

_____

_____

_____

Renewing our mind with tools that allow us to share God's worth is part of this weapon. Guarding our mind is also deciphering the truth from fiction. There is a barrage of information coming at us from every direction. It is incumbent upon us to fill our mind with what is right and pure. It is therefore our role to share that with our children and not just wear a cross around our neck.

We know BE 12 helps protects our brain. How do your values alert you that arrows are flying your way? Which values do you use to shield those arrows? How are you exercising your brain? What key values do you need for salvation? What is your sword that the Holy Spirit has given you?

_____

_____

_____

*"And **pray** in the Spirit on all occasions with all kinds of prayers and requests."*

Above all else, pray! I love how Paul ends this charge with the power of prayer. We can have the strongest armor, and we will never win the war against evil schemes without prayer. You can dig deeper about BEing prayerful in value number eleven.

Prayer:

_____

Grateful Gift:

_____

Week 2

BE Peaceful

Do not worry then, saying, "what will we eat? Or "what will we drink" or "What will we wear for clothing?" For the Gentiles eagerly seek all these things. For your heavenly father knows that you need all these things. But seek first his Kingdom and all His righteous and all these things will be added to you. Matthew 6:25

ANXIETY AND STRESS ARE WRECKING OUR lives. Anxiety disorders affect forty million people above the age of eighteen. Twenty-five percent of children between thirteen and eighteen years old have anxiety disorders. Depression is the leading cause of disability worldwide. Anxiety, as with most mental health illnesses, is treatable. These statistics are frightening and it requires us to recognize the signs and be ready to mobilize.

Finding peace among anxiety may be one of the most challenging journeys you will ever take. Action is the enemy of anxiety so let us talk about how we can find peace in thoughtful activities. I learned in talking to many women, that the comparison trap was a leading cause of anxiety and stress. So, what does it mean to be content with what we have and not compare our life, our beauty and our family to others? For me, it was Philippians 4:12-13

> *"I know what it is to be in need and I know what it is to have plenty. I have learned the secret of being content in any and every situation, whether well fed or hungry, whether living in plenty or in want." Philippians 4:12-13*

For you mothers seeking peace among chaos and stress, let's be honest. It is harder than anyone ever told us. I am raising ladies, not babies. There is a special place in heaven for mothers that survive the hell of raising teenage girls. Don't misunderstand, my daughters are great girls, but the pains of parenting are often indescribable. I am a working mother who has measured herself against the moms in their yoga pants who bake the homemade goods and sew the 100 sequins on the Halloween costumes. I have driven five hours from a meeting with the Governor to attend a poetry coffee house, only to kick another mother out of my seat. I'd rather not relive that episode. I have been jealous of the mother who seems to have the perfect child, husband, hair, and house.

When you are filled with fear, it is difficult to be at peace. As our daughters approached their next chapter and prepared to leave home for college, I was daily wrapped in insecure thoughts. I feared that I failed to teach them life's most important lessons. I became quite the whirling dervish over several months during our oldest daughter's senior year. Meditation, yoga and prayer along with great music helped me thrive. Sisters, please take a minute where you are right now and listen to this song: "*Your Words*" by Third Day. May you hear God's words above all the noise and distractions.

I pray the activities this week will help you find peace.

DAY 1

"Peace I leave with you, my peace I give you. I do not give to you as the world gives. Do not let your hearts be troubled and do not be afraid." John 14:27

MANY OF US MAY BE IN THE FIGHT OF OUR lives. If we are not right now, we may have been, or we might be in the future. My dearest friends have gone through sickness, infidelity, unimaginable challenges with their children, alcoholism, and have sought God to provide peace. James 1:2 says to consider it joy when trials come our way. This is not God trying to be funny; it is God's way of saying He is working in our lives for good. This joy is knowing God is in control. We do not have to be eloquent in our prayers. We have to let go and let God. Ask Him to give you peace and joy and that your heart may be filled with joy. Where do you need peace in your life today? How does God continue to provide you calm and comfort?

_____

_____

_____

_____

Prayer:

_____

Grateful Gift:

_____

Day 2

"Come to me all who are weary and burdened and I will give you rest. Take my yoke upon and learn from me for I am gentle and humble in heart and you will find reset. For my yoke is easy and my burden light."
Matthew 11:28

ARE YOU WEARY TODAY? ARE YOU BURDENED? Before my "spell," I was carrying many heavy yokes that included controlling situations with my friends and family. Recall earlier when we referenced The book *StrengthsFinder 2.0*. My top strengths are futuristic, learner, strategic and command. I am inspired by what could be and desire for continuous improvement. My pitfall is that too often I try to insert my opinion and 'fix' situations. Dissect the above scripture with me. A yoke is typically that which is put on two oxen or cows to evenly distribute the load, thus making it lighter and easier to carry. God will lighten our load when we trust and have peace in his grace.

Are there people trying to help you lighten the load? Is it difficult for you to accept their help?

Describe what burdens you are bearing today? What do you need to let go so God can share the yoke? How does the Serenity Prayer guide you to peace?

> *God, grant me the serenity to accept the things I cannot change, courage to change the things I can, and wisdom to know the difference.*
> *The Serenity Prayer,* Reinhold Niebuhr

_____

_____

_____

_____

_____

_____

_____

_____

_____

_____

_____

_____

_____

_____

_____

_____

_____

Prayer:

_____

Grateful Gift:

_____

Day 3

"Peacemakers who sow in peace reap a harvest of righteousness." James 3:18

Open your Bible and read James Chapter 3. While it is known as "taming the tongue" chapter, there are so many more lessons on peace in this Scripture. Words can bring joy or strife, and it is up to you to decide.

We are reminded that we are not perfect and that we stumble. Most importantly, we know we *can control* the tongue. It is the smallest part of the body. Just like a horse is controlled by the bit or a ship by a small rudder. Instead of venom, let us speak praise.

How can you BE peaceful in your words today? Does it help to pause before you speak? Do you need to write down messages if you anticipate a heated discussion? What does it truly look like to sow peace?

I leave you with two sayings to support you this week. Read them and decide how you can BE more peaceful if you abide by them.

It is better to be loving than right.

If you can't say anything nice, don't say anything at all.

_____

_____

_____

_____

_____

_____

_____

_____

_____

_____

_____

_____

_____

_____

_____

_____

_____

_____

_____

_____

Prayer:

_____

Grateful Gift:

_____

Day 4

"For where you have envy and selfish ambition, there you find disorder and every evil practice." James 3:16

OPEN YOUR BIBLE AND READ JAMES, CHAPTER 3 and soak in its lessons. Whose life are you envious of, and is that productive? Why are you wasting time worrying about someone else's gifts, house, kids? God made them, and God made you.

I was reflecting on the many times I have looked at others' lives and questioned myself. Every time I go to that dark forest, I get lost in insecurity, question my decisions, and choose sadness over joy. I become unorganized in my thinking and even start looking for the negative in those people. *Stop*! My trick is to stop and write down my blessings in my Grateful Journal. I realize my list is long. The beauty is how peaceful and refreshed I feel.

Do you allow these envious and selfish thoughts to block your peace? What are your weak points and vulnerable spots? How do you pull yourself up from the valley?

Prayer:

Grateful Gift:

DAY 5

"The Lord bless you and keep you, the Lord make
his face shine on you and be gracious to you; the
Lord turn his face toward you and give you peace."
Numbers 6:24-26

OUR LORD HAS BLESSED YOU, AND HE SMILES
at you. His grace surpasses our understanding when we sin.
We can spread the peace He has given us, but we need to be
filled with that peace.

Look around you for smiles today. How many do you
see? BE the change today and smile at everyone you see.
Look the person God created right in front of you in the
eye, watch how they will reciprocate.

_____

_____

_____

Reflect on the values we discussed, and talk about how
you have BEen a peaceful servant.

_____

_____

Prayer:

_____

Grateful Gift:

_____

Week 3

BE Patient

"Be still and know that I am God." Psalm 46:10

I SPENT A LIFE OF BEING IMPATIENT, NOT LIS-tening and rushing to the next activity. I pursued the next shiny penny, and beat myself up if I didn't make it a quarter in thirty days. I hurt people and relationships.

My daughters and being a mother taught me the value of patience. The stages of development are moments to savor. When the girls were babies, I followed them around, making sure they didn't swallow quarters or put their finger in electric switches. In elementary school, I was consumed with their learning milestones. In middle school, we fought the evils of social status, comparison, and electronics. Then, in high school, a whole new world emerged. Each stage was a season complete with frigid moments and warm sunshine. If you are in any of these seasons, BE patient, listen and just BE. Good or bad, the season will be gone before you take off your coat.

I am committed to BEing more patient. Because of my commanding, fixer strengths, I needed help to just BE. After a few months as a whirling dervish, tackling people at work, spreading negative energy, and losing my way, I randomly opened my Bible to this Scripture in Psalm 46.

This Scripture was the impetus for the title of this book. I was lost in the hustle and bustle of the day's demands and was losing track of BEing me. The trials and tribulations that God sent my way in those two years spoke to me about waiting for His will.

BE still and know that I am God.
BE still and know that I am God
BE still and know
BE still
BE

DAY 1

Consider it pure joy my brothers and sisters when-
ever you face trials of any kinds, because you know
that the testing of your faith develops perseverance.
Perseverance must finish its work so that you may BE
mature and complete, not lacking anything. If any
of you lacks wisdom, he should ask God, who gives
generously to all without finding fault and it will be
given to him. But when he asks, he must believe and
not doubt, because he who doubts is like a wave of the
sea, blown and tossed by the wind. James 1:2-6

PURE JOY! THAT IS NOT EXACTLY WHAT I FELT
during my lost year nor when I face the challenges of being a
good parent or wife or daughter or sister. What I do understand better today is the power of perseverance. Do you feel
tossed by the wind and crashing waves? How can you BE
still and wait?

_____

_____

_____

_____

Prayer:

_____

Grateful Gift:

_____

Day 2

Bearing fruit in every good work, growing in the knowledge of God, being strengthened with all power according to his glorious might so that you may have great endurance and patience and joyfully giving thanks to the Father, who has qualified you to share in the inheritance of the saints in the kingdom of light. For he has rescued us from the dominion of darkness. Colossians 1:10b-13a

THINK OF A TIME YOU HAVE BEEN RESCUED from the dominion of darkness. How did your patience in God lead you to a brighter place?

Our good work and knowledge in God is strengthened in the challenges because we seek Him and wait for him to provide. What was your darkness and did you seek others to help you?

_____

_____

_____

_____

_____

Prayer:

_____

Grateful Gift:

_____

Day 3

*"Fruits of the Spirit are love, joy, peace, **patience**, kindness, goodness, faithfulness, gentleness, and self-control." Galatians 5:22-23*

OH, TO POSSESS A FEW OF THESE NINE QUALIties. They are woven together and even if we can practice a few every day, we will BE a BEtter person.

Name situations that challenge your patience. You are stuck in traffic. Your child isn't ready and you are running late. Your boss is late for the meeting and likely to make you late to pick up your child. You have to pick up a few items from the grocery store and you are in the longest line. The server messed up your food and now you are late for your next appointment. The Uber driver takes the longest route. Could some of these have been prevented? Maybe. It is not always the outcome, but the process that needs our attention. Describe a situation today or this week where you lived out the fruits of the spirit.

Love _____

_____

Joy _____

_____

Peace _____

_____

*Patience*_____

_____

*Kindness*_____

_____

*Goodness*_____

_____

*Faithfulness*_____

_____

*Gentleness*_____

_____

*Self-Control*_____

_____

Prayer:

_____

Grateful Gift:

_____

Day 4

"Rejoice in hope, be patient in tribulation, be constant in prayer." Romans 12:12

DURING MY REBUILDING YEAR, I SPENT TIME volunteering at homeless and abuse shelters, food pantries and animal rescue centers. Every day there was a new story of hope and faith that grounded me and opened my eyes to BEing focused on others. Stories of women who were physically and emotionally abused with nowhere to go. They had children and no job. There were families who, without the support of Feeding Tampa Bay, would not have food. There were devastated animal lovers who had to give up a dying pet.

On our darkest days, we are called to consistently pray and rejoice in the hope that God provides.

What gives you hope? How have you been patient in tribulation? Have you maintained faithful prayer and been patient as you wait for God's answers?

_____

_____

_____

Prayer:

_____

Grateful Gift:

_____

DAY 5

"And let us not grow weary of doing good, for in due season we will reap, if we do not give up." Galatians 6:9

DO YOU FEEL LIKE YOU KEEP DOING GOOD AND others keep taking? Is it hard to keep doing good? Write about a time that you kept serving someone even when it was hard. Describe the process and outcome and what value helped you stay the course.

_____

_____

_____

_____

_____

Reflect on the values we discussed, and talk about how you have BEen a servant, peaceful and patient.

_____

_____

_____

_____

Prayer:

_____

Grateful Gift:

_____

Week 4

Resolve to BE Mary and Martha

As Jesus and his disciples were on their way, he came to a village where a woman named Martha opened her home to him. She had a sister called Mary, who sat at the Lord's feet listening to what he said. But Martha was distracted by all the preparations that had to be made. She came to him and asked, "Lord, don't you care that my sister has left me to do the work by myself? Tell her to help me!". "Martha, Martha," the Lord answered, "you are worried and upset about many things, but few things are needed—or indeed only one. Mary has chosen what is better, and it will not be taken away from her." Luke 10:38-42

OH, HOW I YEARN TO BE MARY SITTING AT Jesus' feet. The tale of two sisters hits home in many of our daily lives. We are busy preparing, serving, and doing good. I love this whole scene. Martha is making sure the house is clean, the table set, the flowers perfect. Then she boldly says to Jesus, "fix" it. While Jesus rebukes Martha, He is not saying her work is bad, He is saying she was distracted by unimportant things.

This week, as we reflect on being a servant, peaceful and patient, think about when you are Mary or Martha. I am not trying to make myself feel better by saying Martha wasn't so bad; I am BEing practical and honest. Because, sister, I think we are similar in many ways. In our time together this year, we have learned that values must be nurtured and developed. I pray that we sit as Mary did at Jesus' feet and listen, that we serve like Martha and the discernment to know the difference.

Day 1

Think today about serving others, and describe a time when you were BEing Martha and busy with preparation. How did you incorporate Mary into your Martha activities?

_____

_____

_____

Day 2

Today, sit at Jesus' feet and listen. Imagine yourself in a room with Jesus while other activities are going on around you. How are you focused on Him and what is your conversation? Try a day of not BEing busy and unfocused. Use today in prayer, reflection, and be calm.

_____

_____

_____

Day 3

With which sister do you identify the most? Mary or Martha, and why?

_____

_____

_____

Day 4

With which sister would you rather identify? What would need to change for you to BE more like her? Why are both important?

_____

_____

_____

Day 5
Value Assessment Day

Today is your day of reflection. Look back on your notes. What were the most BE moments of this past month? What did you learn about BEing a servant, peaceful and patient?

_____

_____

_____

BE FUN

BLESSED BEYOND MEASURE.

BE Fun

LET US LAUGH, SING, AND DANCE. THESE create positive emotional releases and are tools for building and maintaining relationships. Fun to me is dancing to "Low" by FLOrida in a houseful of teenagers during a sleepover. My daughters still have not forgiven me. Fun is singing and dancing out with friends and belly laughs.

Gal pal, when was the last time you laughed so hard you wet your pants? If it was more than twenty-four hours ago, think about making fun a part of your life. When your solid, loving, kind husband tells you he hasn't seen a smile in months, there is problem! But that was the bomb that told me to get over myself and quit taking myself too seriously. I have learned to keep life simple and to BE fun. I have written the following in my journal and rewrite it at least once a week to remind myself not to take myself too seriously.

Having fun brings joy to you and those around you. As you venture to BE more fun, consider these tricks.

- *Relax and enjoy the moment.*
- *Spend time and pay attention to your friends and family.*
- *Explore and find adventures.*
- *Keep things positive.*

I am not always proud of the way I behave. Too often, I am "on" and in forward motion: my mind thinking of conversations I need to have, things I need to fix, commands I need to bark. So, I have developed a daily commitment to BEing fun. Here are my 5Ls.

I will:

- **Live** in the moment.
- Turn the music up **loud** and sing or dance.
- **Look** for humor around me.
- **Laugh** at myself.
- Do something I **love.**

BE adaptable, joyful, and optimistically positive.

Week 1

BE Adaptable

As I have shared, the *StrengthsFinder* process was quite an eye opening experience for me. It helped me BEtter understand myself and how to BEst interact with others. Adaptability is one of the thirty-four themes and one of my strengths. Author Tom Rath defines it as a flexible person who can stay productive when demands are pulling you in different directions. Demands come in varying forms and will hit us when we least expect them. You may have had a situation that pushed you to adapt. Do any of these sound familiar?

- You lost your job.
- Your husband or partner says he doesn't love you.
- You have lost a spouse or child.
- You daughter calls from school and her boyfriend just broke up with her. . . and you are walking into a critical business meeting.
- Your employee has stolen from the company.
- You're checking out at the grocery and your debit card is denied.
- You have a stroke and need to modify your life.

The easiest thing to do when you are down is stay down. You are *bigger* and BEtter than BEing beaten. Your BEst will show when you are at your worst. Understanding how to BE adaptable is another tool in your tool belt.

DAY 1

For I have learned to be content whatever the circumstances. I know what it is to be in need, and I know what it is to have plenty. I have learned the secret of being content in any and every situation, whether well fed or hungry, whether living in plenty or in want. I can do all things through him who gives me strength. Philippians 4:11-13

ARE YOU TIRED OF BEING SOMETHING THAT you are not? There will always be someone skinnier, smarter, richer, and funnier than you. ***Stop!*** You will be lonely and sad until you memorize this Scripture and live it. Think of your circumstances today and decide where you are on the content scale. Are you in plenty or want? In what ways are you in plenty? In want? Are you hungry for a different life of joy and contentment?

I was complaining to a friend about how folding clothes was boring. In her God-filled way, she said, "Next time, consider how fortunate you and your family are to have clothes."

How about the last sentence in the above Scripture? Oh, and by the way. . . we are reminded we *can do* and BE all things if we trust God's plan.

Prayer:

_____

Grateful Gift:

_____

DAY 2

*"And thou shalt love the Lord thy God with all thine
heart, and with all thy soul, and with all thy might."
Deuteronomy 6:4*

THE BOOK OF DEUTERONOMY INCLUDES FOUR
sermons by Moses and the many hardships he faced over
the forty years that he lead the Israelites from Egypt to the
Promised Land. The Israelites were whiners, complainers,
and lacked faith. Moses pleaded with God again and again
to spare the people, even as they continued to sin.

Read Deuteronomy, Chapter 34. Explain a time when
you thought God led you to something you wanted and
worked for, but in the end, you didn't get what you wanted.
How did you adapt? How did the disappointment make
you feel? Did Moses enter the Promised Land?

_____

_____

_____

_____

_____

Prayer:

_____

Grateful Gift:

_____

Day 3

*For everything there is a season, and a time for every
matter under heaven: a time to be born, and a time
to die; a time to plant, and a time to pluck up what is
planted; a time to kill, and a time to heal; a time to
break down, and a time to build up; a time to weep,
and a time to laugh; a time to mourn, and a time
to dance; a time to cast away stones, and a time to
gather stones together; a time to embrace, and a time
to refrain from embracing. Ecclesiastes 3:1-8*

IN LESS THAN FIVE YEARS, I LOST SOME OF THE
most important people in my life to death. There were days
I wasn't sure I could get out of bed. Keep reading the above
Scripture and know there is a season and a reason for everything. I did.

Describe a time that something happened in your life
that did not seem to fit the Ecclesiastes Scripture.

_____

_____

_____

_____

Prayer:

_____

Grateful Gift:

_____

DAY 4

"You have made known to me the paths of life; you will
fill me with joy in your presence." Acts 2:28

ADAPTABLE OR FLEXIBLE PEOPLE HAVE PLAN B,
C, D, and so on. To be adaptable, you must be resourceful
and look for many solutions. You can see that one size does
not fit all.

When my mom moved in with us after the accident, I
had a great opportunity to modify my daily lifestyle so that
I could BEtter serve her.

Explain a situation where you had to be adaptable.
What values did you use and what was the outcome?

_____

_____

_____

_____

_____

_____

_____

_____

Prayer:

_____

Grateful Gift:

_____

Day 5

"Satisfy us in the morning with your unfailing love,
that we may sing for joy and be glad all our days."
Psalm 90:14

BEING ADAPTABLE REQUIRES YOU NOT TO
blame or complain. If your first plan doesn't succeed, what
is your first reaction? Do you find excuses? Do you look
for others to blame? Do you whine and complain about all
the reasons your attempt didn't succeed? BE honest about
a time when you could have BEen more adaptable. If you
had to move on to Plan B, C, or D, how did you handle it?

_____

_____

_____

_____

_____

_____

_____

_____

Prayer:

_____

Grateful Gift:

_____

Week 2

BE Joyful

"A happy heart is like good medicine and a joyful mind causes good healing." Proverbs 17:22

As I write this, suicide rates have climbed dramatically. Suicide rates have increased in almost every US state in the past twenty years and some states have seen more than a thirty percent increase. The Centers for Disease Control reported that suicide accounted for nearly 45,000 deaths in 2016. The most common reasons that cause suicidal thoughts are grief, sexual abuse, financial problems, remorse, rejections, unemployment, and depression.

These statistics keep me up at night and scare me. I pray that you, my dear sister, will use this book to help yourself or a friend. A friend who lost her husband to suicide shared a simple statement with me: "Mind your mind." While this sounds so easy, it is not. To elaborate on her point, she reminded me we chose joy. No one else can make us happy or sad.

My burning bushes have brightened my path on many roads. One was when I read an article about Happiness 101 at Yale University. Dr. Laura Santos, who identified the high stress and lack of happiness at Yale, developed a curriculum that has gone viral. Santos' course, "Psychology and The Good Life," is the most popular course at Yale. I believe God, who is the source of my happiness, is in six of the main lessons:

1. Spend time and energy in the right way.
2. Take time to express gratitude.
3. Do something nice for someone else and talk with others.
4. Find time to be mindful.
5. Get plenty of exercise and sleep.
6. Practice these every day.

Day 1

"BE joyful always, pray continually, and give thanks in all circumstances, for this is God's will for you in Christ Jesus." 1 Thessalonians 5:16

WHILE I AM A POLLYANNA, I KNOW WE CANNOT always be joyful. In our first month together, we started a grateful journal and we began writing down daily grateful gifts. Review and reflect on what you have written and how this new daily task has helped you BE your BEst.

_____

_____

_____

_____

_____

_____

_____

_____

_____

_____

Prayer:

_____

Grateful Gift:

_____

DAY 2

"Rejoice in the Lord always. I will say it again: Rejoice.
Let your gentleness be evident to all." Philippians 4:4-5

I HAVE BEEN CALLED MANY THINGS OVER THE years. One boss referred to me as the velvet sledgehammer. Other adjectives include: tough, strong, passionate, controlling, and demanding with unrealistic expectations. Gentleness hasn't been one I have heard. Describe how your rejoicing in the Lord spreads your gentleness.

_____

_____

_____

_____

_____

_____

_____

_____

_____

_____

Prayer

_____

Grateful Gift:

_____

Day 3

"So, whether you eat or drink, or whatever you do, do all to the glory of God." 1 Corinthians 10:31

WHAT IS IMPORTANT? WHOSE OPINION IS important? Why do we value so many people's opinions and often let their opinions outweigh ours? Take out a notecard and write down those people whose opinions are most important. Now look at it again. The names should be able to be reflected on a Post-It note. We cannot please or serve everyone. Who are the most fun people in your life? What activities do you do with them that is fun? Talk about some of your most fun times in the last 2 years.

_____

_____

_____

_____

_____

_____

Prayer:
_____

Grateful Gift:
_____

Day 4

"Let them praise his name with dancing, making melody to him with tambourine and lyre!"
Psalm 149:3

DANCING IS HEALING. WHETHER OR NOT YOU played ring around the rosy when your kids were toddlers, your first dance at your wedding, or dancing with friends to your favorite music, it is *fun*. You don't have to be dancing queen good, you just have to feel the music.

My dear friend Debbie is a dancing queen. Not only do we dance to Sister Sledge in the kitchen, but she competes in ballroom dancing. She didn't have time to dance when she was caring for her dying husband Ken. After he died, it took almost two years to start dancing again. She is filled with joy and energy.

What has been a sad time of your life? How do you praise God during this time?

_____

_____

_____

_____

Prayer:

_____

Grateful Gift:

_____

Day 5

"And there you shall eat before the Lord your God, and you shall rejoice, you and your households, in all that you undertake, in which the Lord your God has blessed you." Deuteronomy 12:7

SUCCESS IS THE ABILITY TO CREATE THE LIFE you want. Are you too positive to be doubtful, too optimistic to be fearful, and too determined to be defeated? How does your optimism help you reach the success you want in life?

_____

_____

_____

_____

_____

_____

_____

_____

_____

Prayer:

_____

Grateful Gift:

_____

WEEK 3

BE OPTIMISTICALLY POSITIVE

"Do everything without complaining or arguing."
Philippians 2:14

OPTIMISTIC AND POSITIVE: I LOVE THESE
words. As an adjective, "optimistic" is expecting the BEst
in all possible ways while "positive" is something capable of
BEing affirmed, something real or actual. If you are serious
about purpose, joy, and BEing your BEst, you must let go of
negative energy. So, let us be "optimistically positive."

Science suggests our well-being also is influenced by
the company we keep. Researchers have found that certain
health behaviors appear to be contagious and that our social
networks in person and online can influence obesity, anxiety, and overall happiness. Even exercise routines have been
found to be strongly influenced by our social networks.

Massive research exists around happiness and thinking
positively. Research from Michigan State University found
that strong relationships with family and friends are tied
to higher levels of health and happiness. Every thought in
your brain releases chemicals. BEing focused on negative
thoughts effectively zaps the brain of its positive force-
fulness, slows it down, and can go as far as dimming your
brain's ability to function, even creating depression. On

the flip side, thinking positive, happy, hopeful, optimistic, joyful thoughts decreases cortisol and produces serotonin, which creates a sense of well-BEing. This helps your brain function at peak capacity.

Happy thoughts and positive thinking, in general, support brain growth, as well as the generation and reinforcement of new synapses, especially in your prefrontal cortex (PFC), which serves as the integration center of all of your brain-mind functions. The PFC allows you to control your emotional responses through connections to your deep limbic brain. The PFC is the only part of your brain that can control your emotions and behaviors and helps you focus on whatever goals you elect to pursue. It helps you grow as a human BEing, change what you wish to change, and live life the way you decide!

I am well aware there are dark days when the half-full glass has broken. Yet, when we expect the BEst and live our lives to look for the best, we just might find it. If you're looking for something negative, you will find it. So, look the other way.

DAY 1

**Your thoughts form your character.
Thoughts BEcome actions, so think positively.**

I LOVED WORKING FOR ORLANDO HEALTH AND
the friends and community in Central Florida. In 2001,
God had different plans. Sean and I moved our one-month
old daughter to Belleair, Florida. I commuted to Orlando
for about a year and then was fortunate to keep working
with them in a new capacity when I started my company. I
was not the most optimistic person around our house. My
burning bush was when my wonderful husband said he
hadn't seen me smile in months. And sisters, I had everything to smile about.

Are you living an optimistically positive life? How? If
not, what is keeping you from joy?

_____

_____

_____

_____

_____

Prayer:

_____

Grateful Gift:

_____

Day 2

Finally, brothers, whatever is true, whatever is honorable, whatever is just, whatever is pure, whatever is lovely, whatever is commendable, if there is any excellence, if there is anything worthy of praise, think about these things. What you have learned and received and heard and seen in me—practice these things, and the God of peace will be with you. Philippians 4:8-9

Negative thinking has been proven to BE unhealthy. A 2009 study from the journal, *Circulation*, looked at data from nearly 100,000 women. They found that cynical participants are more likely to have heart disease. Research showed that anger, hate, resentment, hurt, guilt, fear, and vengeance can cause heart disease/stroke, high blood pressure, poor digestion, lessened ability to absorb nutrients, reduced immunological defenses, headache, back pain, fatigue, and sleep disorders. During my "lost year", I had all of these.

When has a negative time in your life literally made you sick?

God answered my prayers and led me to peace and big changes. It was painful and required absolute positive thinking. I took a new approach to the world by seeking what was pure and lovely. I found it in my family and community. I had to look in my village and find who could help me. Who is in your village? Are they positive thinkers? Describe changes you may need to make to think more positively.

_____

_____

_____

_____

_____

_____

_____

_____

_____

_____

_____

_____

_____

_____

_____

_____

Prayer:

_____

Grateful Gift:

_____

Day 3

"A joyful heart is good medicine, but a crushed spirit dries up the bones." Proverbs 17:22

DEATH WAS PREVALENT IN MY LIFE FOR AT LEAST ten years. Each time I lost one of my value-focused family members, I felt like a piece of me was gone. I went through anger and denial. I asked God "why" many more times than I thanked Him. Even though I was surrounded with loving people, I felt alone. I was only looking in and not out. With the support of friends, lots of motivational and grieving books and open communication about my loss, I learned to choose a joyful heart. I found that true joy will soothe the aches and pains of life. REJOICE!!!! Again, I say **REJOICE!**

What does a joyful heart look like to you? How have you overcome a crushed spirit? What healing actions do you take to fully live the value of optimistically positive? .

_____

_____

Prayer:

_____

Grateful Gift:

_____

Day 4

"Walk with the wise and become wise, for a companion of fools suffer harm." Proverbs 13:20

LOOK AT YOUR VILLAGE AND NAME THE PEOPLE and how you need them to BE your BEst. Who are your friends? What joys and accomplishments have your shared with them?

_____

_____

_____

_____

_____

_____

_____

_____

_____

_____

_____

Prayer:

_____

Grateful Gift:

_____

Day 5

"God is our refuge and strength, an ever-present help in trouble." Psalm 46:1

DESCRIBE A FAILURE YOU EXPERIENCED. Through what lens did you see the situation? What process did you follow to recover and who helped you? Think about whether you were negative or positive and how you felt. Since we know the strong seek help, describe the people who helped you rise from the failure.

_____

_____

_____

_____

_____

_____

_____

_____

_____

Prayer:

_____

Grateful Gift:

_____

WEEK 4

REJOICE IN THE MOMENT

THE BOOK OF JAMES WAS ANOTHER LIFEBOAT during my "lost year." While I don't wish anyone a "lost year", I can now thank God for those trials. Those twelve months of floundering and failing led to a BEtter me. James begins the book in chapter one, verse one with dedicating his words to the twelve tribes scattered among the nations.

Pull out your Bible and go to the book of James. There are five chapters and we are going to tackle each one each day.

"Consider it pure joy, my brothers, whenever you face trails of man kinds, because you know that the testing of your faith develops perseverance." James 1:2-3

Day 1
Read James, Chapter 1. Write down four truths in this chapter that remind us not to be tossed by the wind and waves. Verse twelve tells us we are blessed when we persevere under trial because when we have stood the test, we will receive what God has promised. What trial are you going through or have you been through that needs these truths?

_____

_____

_____

Day 2

Read James, Chapter 2. This chapter reminds us to avoid favoritism and that we are made complete by faith and deeds. Describe how you put your faith in action with your deeds.

_____

_____

_____

Day 3

Read James, Chapter 3 and comment on the differences and similarities between wisdom and understanding. Describe your selfish ambitions.

_____

_____

_____

Cursing and praising comes from the same mouth and we have the power to keep it in check. James 3:2 reminds us "we all stumble in many ways." Talk about how you keep yourself in check. What 'sets you off' and what are you doing to build this value?

_____

_____

_____

Reflect on verse seventeen, and describe how this fits your call for wisdom. Read this chapter again and describe your tricks for taming your tongue.

_____

_____

_____

Day 4

Chapter four is your homework today. In Value 5, we saw the first verse. The battles come from within us when we are comparing, blaming, and allowing guilt to take over. In those moments, we are not trusting that God will "come near to us" (v. 7). Record the truths you found in Chapter four. How do these impact your values?

_____

_____

_____

Day 5

And today, read James Chapter five. Buckle up, because we end this week with patience in suffering, faithful prayers, and Elijah. Describe your feelings about this chapter. How does it resonate with you?

_____

_____

_____

BE A GOOSE LEADER

Everyone Is Brilliant
At High Tide

BE Strong

*"For I have come down from heaven not to do my will
but to do the will of him who sent me." John 6:38*

JESUS WAS A LEADER. HE HAD A MISSION, GOALS,
and a strategy. Jesus not only empowered the twelve disciples, He invested time to teach them, mentored them and
trusted them. He managed by walking around and allowed
others to serve Him. Jesus wasn't afraid to do the dirty work
or turn over some tables in the temple to make a point. He
was a humble servant who washed others' feet as we read
in John 13:4-5.

Open your Bible to Mark 9:33-37. What speaks to you
in these verses? What questions would you ask Jesus about
what He said?

My competitive spirit was perplexed by verse 35 when
Jesus gathered the twelve and said, "anyone who wants to
be first must be the very last, and servant of all." One message of this passage is that we are called to focus on serving
others. We know what great leaders look like and we have
seen bad leaders. As a leader, I believe Jesus possessed the
BE values we are building.

Growing up in Kentucky, I often saw geese migrating. I was fascinated that they seemed to be so supportive and organized. After more research, I learned these lessons:

- Geese fly in "V" formation, which allows for greater efficiency. The whole flock adds at least seventy-one percent greater flying range than if each bird flew on its own.
  Lesson: When you share a common direction combined with a sense of community, it's easier to reach the destination.

- Whenever a goose falls out of formation, it suddenly feels the drag and resistance of trying to go at it alone and quickly gets back into formation to take advantage of the lifting power of the bird immediately in front.
  Lesson: You don't have to do it alone. There are always others who will help you, support you and advise you. Ask for help!

- When the lead goose gets tired, he rotates back in the wing and another goose flies point.
  Lesson: We all get tired and need to share responsibilities. Share the hard jobs and know when to relax.

- Geese honk from behind to encourage those up front to keep up their speed.

Lesson: Communication is critical! You may need to honk loud from behind so choose your words and the actions that accompany your communication.

- When a goose gets sick, or is wounded, and falls out, two geese fall out of formation and follow him down to help and protect him. They stay with him until he is either able to fly or until he is dead, and then they launch out on their own or with another formation until they catch up with their group.

Lesson: Support and protect your team. The risk you take in helping may lead to finding a new flock.

BE wrong, resilient and BE a mentor.

BE Strong & Wrong

"But for those you hope in the Lord will renew their strength. They will soar on wings like eagles, they will run and not grow weary, they will walk and not be faint." Isaiah 41:10

THE VALUES OF MANY STRONG WOMEN HAVE influenced me. As I looked through my journal and notes from interacting with women, I found some common traits. And Aimee Pestano's tangramwellness.com blog provided a great list of characteristics of strong women. The list includes:

1. Strong women push pass rejection and criticism. They don't let the judgement of others define them.
2. Strong women see creativity as a gift and use it.
3. Strong women put their gut instinct and intuition to work and ask the right questions.
4. Strong women use the past mistakes for wisdom and growth.
5. Strong women who are mothers "do as I say, not as I do."
6. Strong women ask for help.
7. Strong women respect and care for their bodies.
8. Strong women unapologetically say what they mean and mean what they say.
9. Strong women rise from fire and pain with light and love.
10. Strong women are filled with humility not envy as they lift up other women.

I know so many women who have mounted on eagles' wings despite hurricane winds and monsoon rains. On my hardest day, I haven't battled what they have overcome. They include:

- Rosemary was married to an alcoholic and lost her two best friends to tragic deaths.
- Michele, who, after thirty years, found her amazing soul mate and then bravely cared for him as he was dying.
- Aunt Ruth and Debbie who valiantly cared for and survived the deaths of their husbands.
- Recovering alcoholics who are mentoring others to quit the addiction.
- CEOs who left financially rewarding jobs because of harassment.
- Gal pals whose husbands had second lives and affairs.
- Successful women who leave corporate America to pursue their dreams.
- Working mothers who balance flying balls every day.
- And **you!** Because you are reading this book and because you are focused on BEing your BEst.

And strong leaders are willing to BE wrong. Many of my greatest and most humbling moments were when I was wrong. I am a risk taker and decision maker. These 'strengths' often leave me with saying, "I was wrong." Sometimes it's a mistake that needs correcting. Other times it's a moment in time that needs forgiveness and refocus. Every wrong has taught me a lesson about doing the next right thing.

Day 1

"If you falter in times of trouble how small is your strength." Proverbs 24:10

DESCRIBE HOW YOU ARE A GOOSE LEADER. When things are tough, how do you show your strength? When trouble comes and it affects more than just you, how do you serve those around you?

_____

_____

_____

_____

_____

_____

_____

_____

_____

Prayer:

_____

Grateful Gift:

_____

Day 2

"Show me your ways O Lord, teach me your paths, guide me in your truth and teach me. My hope is in you all day long." Psalm 25:4

AS WE SEEK A DISCERNING HEART, WE UNDERstand God can hold our hand on the path as He teaches us. Think about an earthly teacher. What qualities did they have? How were they a role model? What did they teach you about being wrong? Describe a situation when you were wrong and what you learned. How did this situation help others to grow?

_____

_____

_____

_____

_____

_____

_____

_____

Prayer:

_____

Grateful Gift:

_____

DAY 3

"Finally, be strong in the Lord and in the strength of his might." Ephesians 6:10

WHAT IS YOUR MOST VULNERABLE SPOT, AND how do you rise strong? Do you struggle with being wrong?

I painfully shared mine with you. It stings sharp and hard when people correct my vocabulary and even my actions. Acknowledge your spots here and describe how you are rising strong.

_____

_____

_____

_____

_____

_____

_____

_____

_____

Prayer:

_____

Grateful Gift:

_____

Day 4

Do not let your hearts be troubled. You believe in God, believe also in me. My Father's house has many rooms; if that were not so, would I have told you that I am going there to prepare a place for you? And if I go and prepare a place for you, I will come back and take you to be with me that you also may be where I am. John 14:1-4

MERE MORTALS WILL TRY TO BEAT YOU DOWN. Circumstances will seek to crush you. BElieving that the future is bright and shaking off the negative ropes that hold you down gives strength. The Lord is your helper who can give you wisdom when you ask in prayer and when you believe He is preparing a place for us.

When I read this Scripture, I picture the massive divinity of great "rooms" filled with joy.

What does this metaphor mean to you? What places on heaven and Earth is God preparing for you? What tools do you use to give you confidence in God's blessings? Describe what being strong means to you?

_____

_____

Prayer:

_____

Grateful Gift:

_____

Day 5

"So, we say with confidence, 'The Lord is my helper; I will not be afraid. What can mere mortals do to me?'"
Hebrews 13:6

TAKE A MINUTE TO LISTEN TO THE SONG "*CRY Out to Jesus*" by Third Day. You may noticed the theme that music gives me life. This song kept me afloat after Mignon, Ruth, Daddy, and Uncle Billy's deaths.

God knows our burdens and broken hearts. He gives us healing and grace. Sometimes BEing strong means singing your loudest and crying out for help. You are not alone and you do not need to be afraid.

In 2018, loneliness evolved as a national health threat. Not to be confused with being alone, loneliness is disconnection, depression, and often an overwhelming feeling of loss. According to AARP's Loneliness Study, approximately 42.6 million adults over age forty-five in the United States are estimated to be suffering from chronic loneliness.

Many women are great at helping and not so great at seeking help. If you think a friend is lonely or depressed, BE strong and offer to help them. When people are lonely, they do dangerous and risky things. Describe your true friends and list their names below. How do they bring out the best in you? Good friends are those that you share your hopes and dreams, struggles, and pains. Don't be a statistic; BElieve in the value of true friendship.

_____

_____

_____

_____

_____

_____

_____

_____

_____

_____

_____

_____

_____

_____

_____

_____

_____

_____

_____

Prayer:

_____

Grateful Gift:

_____

Week 2

BE Resilient

You may think it's odd to discuss resiliency with leadership values. Yet, as I reflect, every good leader I know has an incredible power to bounce back. My years working in the healthcare industry helped me better understand resiliency. The heroes and heroines we call nurses, doctors, surgeons, and technicians can save a life in one minute and share bad news in the next. They are resilient because they are confident in their skills and have done all they can for the BEst outcome.

If you are a parent, I can guarantee you have learned resiliency. If you're like me, your daughter has rolled her eyes at you and made you feel like you are ignorant. While parenting can be a confidence killer, the challenges and rewards make us more resilient.

Think about the challenges you have tackled this year. To be resilient or 'bounce back' as some would say, requires utilizing your strengths. Do any of the below traits of resilient people describe you?

- Are concerned about other people;
- Understand their skills and how to use them;
- Keep going, even with they are afraid;
- Keep working on their goals—especially after setbacks; and

- Take risks.

The starfish, or sea star, has been my symbol of resiliency. Consider the connections between women and this unique creature.

- Sea stars have eyes at the end of each arm. It is so obvious that women have depth of sight beyond our eyes, often reflected in our keen sense of "gut" instinct we can "see" something before it happens. If something doesn't seem right, question it. Listen to your intuition.
- They are important predators whose eating habits control the shallow ecosystem. They eat almost anything, hence maintaining the integrity of the shallow ecosystem. Think about your ecosystem. While I do eat almost anything, that is not the comparison here. Your predatory habits make sure you protect your team, your friends, and your family.
- They communicate through touch. We know how a hug, holding a hand or a pat on the back goes a long way to saying "atta girl."
- There are over 2,000 species of sea stars and they are bright, beautiful, and all sizes. Relish who you are because we are beautiful in all sizes and shapes.
- Here is the kicker: they can regenerate a leg. It takes about a year, but they do it.

The sea star doesn't die like the spider when they lose a leg. Even though we might think we are dead after our husband has been unfaithful, or we lose a job, or we find that friend was no friend at all, we can stand on our new, maybe stronger leg. We ladies grow a new, stronger leg and we reinvent ourselves.

Day 1

"Blessed is the man who remains steadfast under trial,
for when he has stood the test he will receive the crown
of life, which God has promised to those who love him."
James 1:12

THE GREEK WORD FOR TRIAL MEANS 'TO PROVE
by testing.' And many translations of steadfast is inter-
changed with endurance. List your strengths below, and
describe how they have helped you tackle challenges
when you have been tested. How did God bless you at the
mountaintop?

_____

_____

_____

_____

_____

_____

_____

_____

_____

_____

_____

Prayer:

_____

Grateful Gift:

_____

Day 2

*"We are afflicted in every way, but not crushed; per-
plexed, but not driven to despair; persecuted, but
not forsaken; struck down, but not destroyed." 2
Corinthians 4:8-9*

During my "lost year", I felt crushed
every day. I felt persecuted, dumb, and not valued. I let
it carry to every part of my life. I missed valuable family
and friend time and vowed when I came out of the valley,
I would value others like never before. I vowed to connect
and reconnect with people just because. I now know the
difference between meaningful and transactional relationships. I was in bed, unable to sleep, trying to meditate, and
I kept having visuals of me shaking myself into shape. I
opened my Bible to the above verse. With God's love and
grace, I cannot be destroyed.

Failure is okay and teaches us our best lessons. Read the
above verse again, and talk about what crushes you? How
do you fight the urge to feel destroyed and instead 'grow
a new leg'?

_____

_____

_____

_____

_____

_____

Prayer:

_____

Grateful Gift:

_____

DAY 3

*"Come to me, all who labor and are heavy laden, and
I will give you rest." Matthew 11:28*

SOMETIMES WE JUST NEED A QUIET, SPECIAL
place to BE still and think.

I was given a painting from one of my mentors which
still serves as a great reminder. It said, "You can have it all,
just not at the same time."

Are you trying to balance too much? Are you taking
care of yourself? Are you running from meeting to meeting?
What is filling your time and is it weighing you down or
lifting you up? Describe your burdens and how you will
commit to "rest."

_____

_____

_____

_____

_____

_____

_____

Prayer:

_____

Grateful Gift:

_____

Day 4

Humble yourselves, therefore, under the mighty hand of God so that at the proper time he may exalt you, casting all your anxieties on him ... And after you have suffered a little while, the God of all grace, who has called you to his eternal glory in Christ, will himself restore, confirm, strengthen, and establish you. 1 Peter 5:6-10

I AM THANKFUL FOR BRENE' BROWN. SHE IS brilliant, a focused researcher, masterful storyteller, bestselling author, mom, and wife. Reading any of her books may change the way you look at yourself and others. In her book, *Rising Strong*, she describes a three-phase process to use when rising from setbacks. Her three phases are reckon, rumble, and revolutionize.

Read 1 Peter 5:6-10. Describe a recent setback or one that you are still experiencing. Take a lot of time today to figure out your emotions. What is the impact of this situation on your life? Who else is affected? Spare no words or feelings, describe the setback, how you came to terms with it, fought it, and then rose above it.

_____

_____

_____

_____

_____

_____

Prayer:

_____

Grateful Gift:

_____

Day 5

THIS WEEK, YOU DUG DEEP WRITING ABOUT trials, tests, failures, and how you bounced back. As you reflected on these, what strengths do you BElieve helped you BE your BEst? Trusting your gut is a skill women possess, especially in turmoil. How was your faith tested in these challenges, and what scripture helped you bounce back stronger? Describe the people in your village that you relied on for wisdom and support.

_____

_____

_____

_____

_____

_____

_____

_____

_____

_____

_____

_____

_____

_____

_____

Prayer:

_____

Grateful Gift:

_____

BE a Mentor and Have a Mentor

"Remember your leaders, who spoke the word of God to you. Consider the outcome of their way of life and imitate their faith." Hebrews 13:7

WE ALL NEED HELP. THE STRONG ASK FOR IT.

There are therapists, church leaders, friends, family, spouses, and others who have wisdom for you. While I cannot stress enough that if you want to truly BE and BE able to care for others, you must take care of yourself. Those who help and serve others find it difficult to ask for help.

Mentors have been a part of my village since my first job. My mentors have been wise and trusted counselors from various walks of life. They have included teachers and confidantes from my family, my church, and the community. I have also had sponsors in the organizations I have worked. In addition to your champions, cheerleaders and advocates, I urge you to find mentors and sponsors. A mentor will recognize your strengths, areas of development and will help you thrive. They use their experiences to guide and direct you. Sponsors are within your organization that openly advocate on your behalf. They help you connect to career opportunities, important assignments, and guide you to building relationships with key leaders of your organization. A sponsor takes a vested interest in your career growth, promotion and future. The keys to successful relationships with mentors and sponsors are trust and consistent communication.

Day 1

"Tell me and I forget, teach me and I may remember,
involve me and I learn." Benjamin Franklin

NAME FIVE PEOPLE IN YOUR WORKPLACE, YOUR industry, or someone you identify as successful in the ways you'd like to BE. Would you like to meet with them? Could they BE a mentor? Circle the top three and find out more about them and if you decide to be brave, call or email them and see if they are available for coffee or tea.

_____

_____

_____

_____

_____

_____

_____

_____

_____

_____

Prayer:

_____

Grateful Gift:

_____

Day 2

Give and it will be given to you. A good measure pressed down, shaken together and running over, will be poured into your lap. For with the measure you use, it will be measured to you. Luke 6:38

Read Luke 6:38 above again and again. When we give, we receive. Sharing our strengths and wisdom with others through mentoring produces overflowing good measures.

Do you have a mentor or sponsor? If you don't, please find one. Look around at people you respect in your field, industry, or interest. I have been fortunate to be supported by great mentors and sponsors. And, there are more I hope to learn from in future years. In college, I had a great Economics professor and the Director of Student Life. My first 'real' job at Fifth Third Bank in Cincinnati paired me with a mentor, Carolyn McCoy, the president of the Fifth Third Bancorp Foundation. She was poised, professional, and so wise. She was instrumental in teaching me about the corporate world as we met every month throughout my career. Over the years, I continued to build a broader village of those that make me BEtter. Describe your support system below. Where are there gaps and how do you fill them?

You may need to take a risk when you ask someone to be your mentor. One action item in my reinvention plan after the 'lost year' included gaining wisdom. That meant being brave to contact people and ask for help. I called a successful local leader named Joe Jimenez and asked if he would be my mentor. I barely knew him. He graciously accepted and he continues to provide honest wisdom, ideas, and support. Find a Joe! He is a kind, unassuming, hard worker, a brilliant marketer, father to two incredible daughters, husband, servant, and above all else, cares about people.

Describe your mentor. How have they helped you? Do you regularly meet with them? If you have not spent time with them recently, connect with them today.

_____

_____

_____

_____

_____

_____

_____

_____

_____

_____

_____

_____

_____

_____

_____

_____

_____

_____

Prayer:

_____

Grateful Gift:

_____

Day 3

"Two are better than one, because they have a good return for their labor. If either of them falls down, one can help the other up. But pity anyone who falls and has no one to help them up." Ecclesiastes 4:9-10

HOPEFULLY, YOU HAVE A MENTOR OR MENTEE. If not, you can use these questions when you obtain one. Here are questions Inc.com provided in regard to mentoring. They are framed for you to ask your mentor and I hope you will. I also hope as you BEcome a mentor that you will use them to help others grow.

- What do you wish you knew at my age?
- Who else would you recommend I connect?
- How can I work smarter?
- If you could do it all again, what would you do differently?
- What are you trying to accomplish this quarter?
- What should keep me up at night? What keeps you up at night?
- What were your biggest failures?
- What has been your most rewarding accomplishment?
- What am I doing wrong?

I have my answers to many of the above in my "sunshine file" to remind me how to BE my BEst. You may want to take a minute to answer some of them.

_____

_____

_____

_____

_____

_____

_____

_____

_____

_____

_____

_____

_____

_____

_____

Prayer:

_____

Grateful Gift:

_____

Day 4

"Show them how to live by your life and by right teaching. You should be wise in what you say. Then the one who is against you will be ashamed and will not be able to say anything bad about you." Titus 2:7-8

MENTORS ARE ROLE MODELS. WHETHER YOU are in a formal mentoring relationships or not, you are a role model to those around you. Your actions and your words are being watched. If you are a parent, think for a minute how your child spoke to their doll, stuffed animal, or each other. Does it sound like a recording of your words?

How do you show your life to others by your actions and your deeds? What have you done recently to share your wisdom by teaching someone? And, look at verse eight— the one who is against you will have to keep their mouth shut. Instead of competing or wondering how those that are against you will attack, focus on your wisdom and teach right.

_____

_____

_____

_____

Prayer:

_____

Grateful Gift:

_____

Day 5

"Great are your purposes and mighty are your deeds. Your eyes are open to the ways of all mankind; you reward each person according to their conduct and as their deeds deserve." Jeremiah 32:19

CARLA HARRIS IS A PHENOMENON. A CAREER Wall Street banker, singer, author and speaker. She brilliantly describes the difference between an advisor , mentor and sponsor. An advisor gives you the answer usually to a specific question. A sponsor is usually within your work organization who may guide you and go to bat for you. A mentor is someone you can trust and tell the good, bad and ugly.

We need all of these, and we can serve in these roles to others. Describe the values of the people who served in these roles for you.

_____

_____

_____

_____

_____

Prayer:

_____

Grateful Gift:

_____

Week 4

REFRESH Your Leadership

I HAVE BECOME CONSUMED WITH THE CONcept of servant leadership. The term was coined by a former AT&T Executive, Robert Greenleaf in 1970 and has taken many forms. For me, servant leadership describes what God has called me to BE and do. The characteristics include; listening, empathy, awareness, commitment to growing people, and building community.

Day 1
Look at the five characteristics, and describe below how you possess them or what you need to do to gain a spirit of servant leadership.

Listening:

_____

_____

_____

Empathy:

_____

_____

_____

Awareness:

_____

_____

_____

Growing people:

_____

_____

_____

Building community:

_____

_____

_____

Day 2

The concept of servant leadership is that you are willing to support the greater good, even if it means sacrificing yourself or ideas. What is an example where you were focused on the greater good? Describe how you used your values to make a change.

_____

_____

_____

_____

Day 3

As you have read BE 12, you have focused on your value system. When it comes to leadership, describe a great leader who has helped form you. Name that person. In what ways did she or he help? What was a situation where you saw their resiliency?

_____

_____

_____

_____

Day 4

How often have you seen strong female leaders labeled as "bossy, controlling," and other choice words? Strong, vocal men who stand up for their position, sometimes at high decibels, are considered a "leader." What type of leader are you? How do you lead in your office or home?

_____

_____

_____

_____

Day 5

Value Assessment

As you review your notes from this month, what values resonate most with you? How will you be strong, wrong, a mentor and resilient?

_____

_____

_____

BE ON PURPOSE

Do What You Love. Love What You Do and Be Really Good at It.

BE On Purpose

WHAT IS YOUR BURNING BUSH? MANY OF MY epiphanies have been in the smoke of a burning bush. I love the story of Moses in Exodus 3. Please read that chapter now and summarize the scene. Describe what you know about Moses' early life that prepared him for leadership.

_____

_____

_____

_____

_____

_____

_____

_____

What is your burning bush? When have there been times that you wanted to run from an epiphany that was calling you? As I wrote this book, I struggled with my calling and looked in the fiery flame of many burning bushes.

Yoga or "Yo God" as I sometimes call it, is one of my passions and has guided me to healing and direction. Yoga helped me cope in the "lost year" and spurred me to calm and peace. I use my yoga time to converse with God. On days that I walk into a yoga class with a headache, I leave soaring like a feather. The breathing techniques promote a sense of peace and joy. Yoga is an inward experience reflective of our BEing. For those of you that have taken a yoga class, I hope you identify with these life lessons. For those that have not, I encourage you to try it.

Breathing gives life. Focused breathing relaxes your heart and clears your head.

Every day and every side presents a new opportunity. The poses in yoga are done on each side of your body. One day, the right side might be tight and the next day, the left. Every day you can feel the chance to improve and the chance to be satisfied. The goal is not struggling to put your nose on the floor, but instead to reach your BEst place.

Nudge past resistance. Each time you reach a new pose, you may feel resistance. Similar to goal-setting, we need to push past barriers to find fulfillment.

Poses are harder when you close your eyes. The same is true of life. When we put on blinders, we lose sight of the facts and stumble.

Balance. Practice, focus, and prioritization are the tools you need to balance the many hats you wear.

Driste! *Driste* is when you lock your eyes on something so to help your balance. It may be used in tree pose to center yourself. You stare at a spot on the wall or anything that will keep you balanced. The power of focus is not to be underestimated. Truly, what it takes to BE balanced is focus. BEing on purpose.

The power of quietness can open your mind to new ideas, so gal pals, let me share one with you. Because yoga has been so beneficial to my walk with God, I set a goal to share it with others. I am praying about **God Yoga or YoGod**, still working on the name. Send me an email if you like the idea and which name you like better. Working with women's conferences, local churches, schools, and business, I'd like to bring yoga to the classroom of life. Imagine a Christian women's conference where women can use an hour in prayer while improving their balance and strength. Or imagine young adults using the time to relax and relieve their minds of stress and anxiety.

BE focused, present, and accountable.

Week 1

BE Focused

"And we know that in all things God works for the good of those who love him, who have been called according to his purpose." Romans 8:28

EVERY YEAR, I WRITE DOWN A WORD OR PHRASE that reflects an area I need to BE BEtter. For two years, the phrase was *focus* and *let God*! Yet, other years are different. God has given me burning bushes to brighten my focus and let *go*.

The Lenten season is a focused growth period for many in the Christian faith. It represents a forty-day preparation before the Holy Easter holiday. I treasure Lent as a time to walk closer in my faith. Too often, Christians deny themselves of chocolate, alcohol, cursing, and other consumption habits. Instead of giving up, Lent is meant for us to give in. We are called to sacrifice for a strong heart.

The Lent season after I turned fifty was a particularly powerful one. My commitment during this season was to listen to God's calling. God gave me all the tools, just like He always does. He gave me daily Scripture, friends, accountable sisters in His love, and then He gave me His miracles. The beginning of Lent 2018 fell on the Wednesday before my mother and daughter's car accident. I wrote down my

Lent commitments and the plan I would follow. I prayed I would let go of my controlling habits and trust God. I knew many of my relationships were suffering and I prayed for direction. Secondly, I needed Him to direct my paths. God delivered miracles. God saved the lives of my mother and daughter. He gave me another chance to serve my mother. And, God gave me people to help me finish this book and refine my calling.

Day 1

"For the Lord God is a sun and shield; the Lord will give grace and glory; no good thing will He withhold from them that walk uprightly." Psalm 84:11

WHAT IS YOUR WORD? WHY IS THIS WORD A growth opportunity and how will you turn it into action? Your period of preparation doesn't have to be in the spring during Lent.

I fast several times a year and it proves to give me a closer walk with God. If you are exploring a fast, the Daniel Fast is a good one. Describe an area of your life that needs more focus.

_____

_____

_____

_____

_____

_____

_____

_____

Prayer:

_____

Grateful Gift:

_____

DAY 2

"I am carrying on a great project and cannot go down."
Nehemiah 6:3

THE BOOK OF NEHEMIAH IN THE OLD
Testament is one of focus, risk, and loyalty. Read Nehemiah
6 and describe Nehemiah, his focus, and his purpose.

How are you similar to him? What project are you
working on right now that you believe God has put in your
hands? Are others trying to stop you? Why?

_____

_____

_____

_____

_____

_____

_____

_____

_____

_____

Prayer :

_____

Grateful Gift:

_____

Day 3

"Let your eyes look straight ahead; fix your gaze directly before you." Proverbs 4:25

IT IS EASY TO TAKE OUR EYES OFF THE PRIZE, especially when things get foggy.

I am addicted to running and swimming. You know swimming has taught me many lessons. I use my time in the pool to pray and center myself. When my goggles get foggy, I don't see the black line and bump into the lane lines. I am reminded we need to pause, reset, and clear our "goggles."

What fogs your vision? Describe times when you have focused your gaze.

_____

_____

_____

_____

These are some tips I have found for being focused:

- Complete projects and activities that require creative thinking and concentration first. Then move to easier work such as deleting emails or organizing them.
- Allocate your time deliberately. Find your spot and time of the day where your productivity is the best.
- Train your mind like a muscle. Turn off all distractions and commit to a single task. Start small with five minutes then build up to more.

Is focus an area you need to grow? How can these tips help? What else will you do to focus on the important not the urgent? Make a list of the important things in your life and urgent fires that you are dealing with this week

_____

_____

_____

_____

_____

_____

Prayer:

_____

Grateful Gift:

_____

Day 4

"Be confident of this, he who began a good work in you will carry it on to completion until the day of Christ Jesus." Philippians 1:6

DESCRIBE A PROJECT OR TASK WHERE YOU ARE obsessed about the outcome. Do you just want to finish the report? Remodel the bathroom? Send your child to college? Are you missing the chance to teach others? To be kind to the contractors? To teach your child about God, a discerning heart and how to serve? It is in the process that we learn how to BE our BEst selves.

_____

_____

_____

_____

_____

_____

_____

Prayer:

_____

Grateful Gift:

_____

Day 5

*"Commit to the Lord what you do, and you will suc-
ceed." Proverbs 16:3*

THIS SCRIPTURE SAT ON MY DESK AS I WROTE
BE 12. There were so many days I wanted to give up. Every
time I prayed to God, "Are you sure this is what you want
me to do?" An answer came whether it was an encouraging
word from my husband or a friend, a stranger, or a speaker
at a conference.

What is a project or task that you have been planning
to do? Why is it important? Do you want to complete it
and do you have the grit to do it? If yes, pray to God and
ask Him to give you the tools to accomplish it.

_____

_____

_____

_____

_____

_____

_____

Prayer:

_____

Grateful Gift:

_____

WEEK 2

BE PRESENT

"But the fruit of the Spirit is love, joy, peace, patience, kindness, goodness, faithfulness, gentleness, self-control." Galatians 5:22-23

THE BIBLE DOES *NOT* TELL US TO BE BUSY. IN today's fast-paced, action-packed lives, we struggle to find calm and peace. You cannot be fruitful when you are drunk on being busy. I pray you will not see it as validation of your worthiness but instead seek to BE present in your thoughts, words and deeds.

For years, I lived a life of running from one activity to the next, one project to another, checking one more email, sending one more text. I did all this because it made me feel important and needed. The dopamine hit from having countless emails, calls, and texts kept me spinning. I missed funerals and friends that were ill or going through a divorce or had a sick child. During my rebuilding year, I hit the brakes hard. For twelve months, I used meditation, yoga, prayer, and these tips for BEing present to BE my BEst.

- *Show up* at funerals, weddings, and birthdays.
- At meals and in meetings, put the phone away. It is rude and you are not paying attention or showing respect.
- Prioritize and be clear about family phone use. Set rules for when they are in the car with you. You will

be amazed what your children say in the car when they aren't looking at you. Your family and others on the road deserve your full attention.

- Know the difference between urgent and important.
- Look people in the eye, clear your mind of distractions and listen.

Day 1

*"A new command I give you; love one another. As I have
loved you, so you must love one another." John 13:34*

JESUS WAS SERIOUS ABOUT LOVING EACH
other. What friends, family, or coworkers are going through
difficult times? Or perhaps they are planning a wedding
or baby shower or having a big birthday. How can you be
supportive? How can you be present? Could you cook
pumpkin bread, plan for a meal to be delivered, or send a
card? Are you planning to attend the birthday party or event
being planned? If you are not, think about why or why not.

Prayer:

Grateful Gift:

Day 2

*"Value others above yourselves, not looking to your own
interests but each of you to the interests of the others."
Philippians 2:4*

You know my family are hard workers
and let me tell you about how they show up. Whenever
someone moves to a new home, they mobilize. Aunt
Ruth, Uncle Billy before he passed, cousins Beth and Ron,
Rosemary, and Michele haul, drive moving trucks, arrange
furniture, hang pictures, clean silver, paint, and hang wall-
paper. They show up in full force. They don't check their
emails or their phones; they just serve.

Describe who and how those in your life "show up."
Who is present in the most critical moments?

_____

_____

_____

_____

_____

_____

_____

Prayer:

_____

Grateful Gift:

_____

Day 3

"Eye hath not seen, nor ear heard, neither have entered into the heart of man, the things which God hath prepared for them that love Him." 1 Corinthians 2:9

THERE ARE 7.5 BILLION PEOPLE IN THE WORLD and 6.8 billion cell phones. Houston, we have a problem. My daddy once commented about my cell phone use: "I bet Johnson didn't have one of those when President Kennedy was shot." I know it is not 1969, but I do know people deserve our respect and maybe, even more today. So, I urge you today, as a woman of character, a role model, and if you are a mother, to establish boundaries. Make decisions and consider a family contract regarding the use of a phone and social media. We need guardrails and guidelines. Today, put your phone away for meetings and meals, unless, of course, you are waiting for an emergency. Since texting is illegal while driving in forty-seven states as of this writing, put your cell phone in the trunk or somewhere you won't be tempted. Establish three to five set times that you will check your texts and emails. Were you more productive, more present, and thinking more clearly?

_____

_____

Prayer:

_____

Grateful Gift:

_____

DAY 4

*"Then they sat on the ground with him for seven days
and seven nights. No one said a word to him, because
they saw how great his suffering was." Job 2:13*

THE STORY OF JOB HAS ALWAYS DISTURBED ME.
I have grown to better understand God's will and how bad
things do happen to good people. Yet, the pain and suffering Job experienced while he kept his faith humbles me.
There is another lesson in Job about friends BEing present.
When Job's three close friends heard of his troubles, they
left everything and went to comfort him.

Describe a time when friends were there for you. Who
are those friends, and how did it teach you to show up
for others?

_____

_____

_____

_____

_____

_____

Prayer:

_____

Grateful Gift:

_____

Day 5

*"Cause me to hear thy lovingkindness in the morning;
for in Thee do I trust; cause me to know the way
wherein I should walk; for I lift up my soul unto thee."
Psalm 143:8*

I READ A STORY OF A MINISTER WHO WAS ON A mission trip for seven days in South America. For six days, a woman came to the altar after the message and asked him to pray to kill the cobwebs in her life. He dutifully prayed with her and each night, she came back, and on day six, he said, "I am praying the wrong prayer. Pray with me: 'Gracious God, *kill* the spider.'

What is building the cobweb in your life? How many times have you walked through a cobweb and felt like the threads were still on your skin and clothes? Are the cobwebs in your life preventing you from BEing your BEst? What are your spiders? Do they need a fast crushing with your shoe or do you need a more deliberate approach to ridding the culprit?

_____

_____

_____

Prayer:

_____

Grateful Gift:

_____

WEEK 3

BE ACCOUNTABLE

"So then, each of us will give an account of ourselves to God." Romans 14:12

GOD CALLED ME, AND I THOUGHT I KNEW better. Gal pals, let me tell you my painful story and how I learned about accountability, owning my circumstance, and BEing my BEst.

Before my "lost year", I had a great job. I was an executive at a not-for-profit, surrounded by brilliant, driven people. The CEO, my boss, was honest and caring and brought out the BEst in me. I had many successes, and then I failed myself and those I worked with. We started a great thing, just like Nehemiah, and instead of fighting for my people, I came down. I created villains and told myself I was the victim. For months, I looked for everything bad and I found it. Instead of choosing joy, I chose sadness. I stormed across lanes like a semitruck. I learned valuable lessons. Instead of me BEing content in my skin, I clawed to be like other people. I did not feel valued and stopped writing my own story. I allowed myself to be wooed away to another organization that "promised" to use my skills. It took me twelve months, therapy, great friends and loving people to understand my mistake.

Society has become one of blaming and making excuses. While it is easy to do, if you keep blaming someone or something, your problems will never go away. Being responsible for your actions is one of the most important steps you can take to BEcoming your BEst self. Which of these traits of accountable people do you have?

- Create a mission statement.
- Set micro goals.
- Use lists wisely.
- Do one task at a time.
- Emphasize your strengths. Improve your weaknesses.
- Set expectations.
- Make success attainable.
- Are role models.
- Take responsibility.
- Don't make excuses.
- Are on time.
- Control their own fate.
- Own their feelings.
- Manage expectations.
- Collaborate.
- Don't expect praise.

That's a long list, so grab three you do well and think of three that need refining. You determine what success looks like, and I believe success results when we do the best with what we have. It is not a random act; it arises out of a predictable set of circumstances and opportunities.

DAY 1

"Everyone is brilliant at high tide." John Ofenloch, MD

PETER WAS A FISHERMAN WHOSE LIFE WAS ONE of great redemption. He gave up his life to follow Jesus and was considered part of the inner circle, as illustrated in Matthew, Chapter 17. He wanted a mighty faith, but like me, faltered often. He plunged into the waves and his doubt registered. He denied Jesus three times, just as predicted.

Once, while boating with our dear friends, the Ofenlochs, and Dr. John, a brilliant surgeon, coined the best phrase as we decided when to head back to the dock. It describes many situations: **everyone is brilliant at high tide**. We are all great when things are going well, but navigating the tide is not for the weak and lazy. The captain must plan when the boat comes in and out of the dock and use tools to check the depth so the boat doesn't run aground.

Describe those moments when all is going great and you've completed an important project and the tide is high. Then, something or someone happens to run you aground. How do you behave? Do you blame or are you accountable to the situation?

_____

_____

_____

_____

_____

_____

_____

Prayer:

_____

Grateful Gift:

_____

Day 2

*"Work for a cause, not for applause. live life to express,
not to impress. Don't strive to make your presence
noticed, just make your absence felt." Unknown*

I HAVE HAD FABULOUS JOBS AND THE PERFECT
one does not exist. What I know is the best job is a combination of your passions, skills, fulfillment, the people, and
the mission of the organization.

How can you BE accountable in using your passions
and skills to find fulfillment?

_____

_____

_____

_____

_____

_____

_____

_____

_____

Prayer:

_____

Grateful Gift:

_____

Day 3

"So, then each of us shall give account of himself to God." Romans 14:12

IF YOU DON'T RECALL THE STORY OF ADAM AND Eve, pause for a few minutes and read Genesis, Chapter 3. While there are many lessons, I want to draw your attention to the blame Adam so quickly throws out. He completely sells out his soulmate, the only gal around. He throws her under the bus without a moment's hesitation.

How often do we blame without gathering the facts? Describe a situation where you were not accountable for your actions. Describe the outcome and how you course corrected.

_____

_____

_____

_____

_____

_____

_____

Prayer:

_____

Grateful Gift:

_____

Day 4

"Oh, that men would praise the Lord for His goodness,
and for His wonderful works to the children of men!
He satisfies the longing soul and fills the hungry soul
with goodness." Psalm 107:8-9

May your "yes" be **"Yes"** and your "no" be
"No." My old self said "yes" too often—all the time. I was so
hungry to serve that I agreed to too much. I was blessed to
serve on many not-for-profit boards, volunteered countless
hours, chaired fundraising events, and attended events several nights a week. I made hard decisions to let my "yes" be
"yes" and "no" mean "no."

A few years later, I went off all the community boards
and committed to serving on one board at a time. I say "yes"
only to activities about which I am passionate and fit our
family's values.

List your activities such as boards, volunteering, book
clubs, that take your time. Describe how they reflect your
values. Acknowledge which ones are stopping you from
BEing your BEst. Describe a change if one is needed,
and own it.

_____

_____

_____

_____

_____

Prayer:

Grateful Gift:

Day 5

THERE ARE MANY STORIES OF THE VICTIM, THE Villain, and the Hero. Wherever there is a victim, there is a villain, and a hero likely emerges. Too often, I created myself in the victim scenario and found villains to blame. We create these scenarios more often than we think.

Do these sound familiar? Maybe your son or daughter fails a test. Have you heard them scream, "That teacher is awful! He doesn't teach me anything!" The teacher is the villain.

A co-worker doesn't finish a project and leaves the team in a lurch. "I didn't have time because we need more staff around here and who knows what our horrible boss wants. She never communicates." No more excuses! Be the hero.

Describe times when you have played victim, villain, and hero. Answer for yourself what you could have done to BE more accountable.

_____

_____

_____

_____

Prayer:

_____

Grateful Gift:

_____

Week 4

Refine Your Purpose

"You would bless me indeed, and enlarge my territory, that your hand would be with me, and that you would keep me from evil." 1 Chronicles 4:10

Day 1

"Now to him who is able to do immeasurably more than all we ask or imagine, according to his power that is at work within us." Ephesians 3:20

While writing this book, the last month was nearly impossible for me. I am passionate about so many things and it is difficult for me to stay on purpose. My interest does not guarantee my success. Prior to finishing this book, I doubted myself regularly. I wrote and wrote, edited, rewrote, and questioned whether I could finish. My deepest dive to finding my purpose was answering these questions.

To BE your BEst, spend as much time as you need to thoughtfully answer these for yourself:

Who are you?

_____

_____

_____

What do you do?

_____

_____

_____

For whom you do it?

_____

_____

_____

How are you changed?

_____

_____

_____

What are you good at?

_____

_____

_____

What do people tell you that you are good at?

_____

_____

_____

What is holding you back?

_____

_____

_____

Day 2

"'For I know the plans I have for you,' declares the Lord,
'plans to prosper you and not to harm you, plans to
give you hope and a future.'" Jeremiah 29:11

Author Steven Covey stresses the importance of our mission statement. Your mission statement needs to define your personal and ethical guidelines that reflect your morals and how you will put it all in action. Your mission statement is how you accomplish your purpose.

For the rest of this week, we are going to refine your mission statement by developing your purpose. Mission drives you and purpose guides you. Looking at the answers to yesterday's questions, start with a purpose statement. This should reflect the person you want to become, not just what you want to have or achieve. All the work we have done to date will help reflect your core values as you create your mission statement. List three to six of your values. Make an action statement for each one. For example, I will be accountable for my actions and choices as I strive to be honest and authentic.

_____

_____

_____

_____

_____

_____

Day 3

Great are your purposes and mighty are your deeds.
Your eyes are open to the ways of all mankind; you
reward each person according to their conduct and as
their deeds deserve." Jeremiah 32:19

Think about the roles you serve. These may include friend, wife, mother, or boss. How do you want to be remembered? Think about the legacy you want to leave behind. For example, she was a compassionate visionary who never met a stranger. Write your legacy.

_____

_____

_____

Day 4

"The Lord works out everything to its proper end."
Proverbs 16:4

Now, write a purpose for each of these elements of your life: physical, mental, emotional, and spiritual. For example: "I respect my body by eating healthy foods and exercising regularly. I am a life-long learner and will read and expand my skills daily. I will serve my family and those in need with focus and dedication. I will daily pray to God, thanking Him and asking Him for wisdom."

_____

_____

_____

Day 5

Now put it all together. It can be two or three paragraphs, bullets, or anything that is easiest for you. When you are finished, post it where you see it and *live it*!

_____

_____

_____

_____

_____

_____

_____

_____

_____

_____

_____

_____

_____

_____

_____

_____

_____

_____

BE RESPECTFUL

There is No Traffic On the High Road

BE Respectful

"I am your brother. But don't be upset and don't be angry with yourselves. God sent me ahead of you to save many lives." Genesis Chapters 44-45.

YOU RECALL THE STORY OF JOSEPH AND HOW his jealous brothers left him for dead. Read Genesis 44-45. Summarize the story here as you describe the values of Joseph, his father, and his brothers.

_____

_____

_____

You can see the values in this book are listed alphabetically. However, if you had to put one forward that can change your life and make the biggest impact on society, it is respect. We need a community conversation about respect.

_____

_____

_____

_____

_____

As I spoke with women, observed, and conducted research into respect, I found many holes. Even though we may each have our own definition, we know what it looks like and we know when it is missing. When we respect someone, we admire them, their qualities, and their achievements. We have a feeling of admiration for them. BEing respectful as a value is putting admiration into action. If you can abide by the golden rule, you can be respectful and put others before yourself.

How often do you hear sayings like "cream rises to the top" or "take the high road"? Do you ever find it's not busy on the high road? When you see others rising to the top, excelling at what looks like great success, does it feel like the nice girl finishes last? How often do we want to mimic their actions thinking their success should be yours? Instead of those lies, these facts are true:

Strong moral character is centered on respect.
Respect is not given, it is earned.
And it starts with respecting yourself.

I presume you can answer "yes" to at least one of the following:

- Have you been ignored when you were talking to someone?
- Have people talked over and interrupted you?
- Have you been bullied?
- Has someone made unsolicited sexual comments or actions to you?

- Have you experienced road rage?
- What type of comments have you made about someone? who doesn't look like you or lives a different lifestyle?
- Have you commented on someone who doesn't look like you?
- Have your children said unkind words to you and rolled their eyes at your direction?

As I observed the most respectful people, the similarities were apparent. They:

- Show gratitude
- Compliment other's achievements
- Look people in the eye
- Speak to others as they want to be spoken to
- Follow the "societal" rules
- Limit complaining
- Yell in their head, not at someone
- Are kind
- If they cannot say anything nice, they DO NOT say anything at all.

**Stay on the High Road! BE a listener,
mannerly, and generous.**

WEEK 1

BE A LISTENER

IN STEVEN COVEY'S *HABITS OF HIGHLY Successful People*, Habit 5 is "Seek First to Understand." All the habits are powerful, but the habit of listening to understand is BEyond valuable. In today's high-tech, high speed world, we seem to spend less time listening to one another. Listening to someone is giving them the gift of your time. Listening builds relationships, resolves conflicts, saves marriages and builds confident kids.

Listening is the most important element of communication. Yet, it's the one at which I fail most often. Empathy is a strength good listeners possess. As I have shared, this is not one that I excel. To BE my BEst, to build stronger relationships, and to illustrate that I cared about people, I had to find any tools to BEcome a better listener. Not listening has threatened many of my relationships. On too many occasions, people I cared about were telling me that I didn't listen and were forced to repeat important information. I am passionate about people so I exercised diligence to improve this value. Listening:

- Illustrates respect
- Improves patience
- Builds trust
- Increases empathy

- Grows the speaker's self-confidence
- Has healing powers
- Makes you a better leader
- You learn new information and skills
- BEcome a better role model

Day 1

*"A wise man will hear and increase in learning. And
a man of understanding will acquire wise counsel."*
Proverbs 1:5

CONSCIOUSLY, PUT AWAY EVERYTHING THAT
could interfere with you listening to everyone with whom
you interact today. List the things you 'put away' as you
may be surprised how small, yet big they are. Look people
in the eye when they are talking to you. Be attentive to their
words. Ask questions without interrupting. Appreciate the
pause and silence as they are talking. Describe what you
learned today by listening? Describe the reactions and
smiles of those you interacted with when they noticed you
were paying attention to them.

_____

_____

_____

_____

_____

_____

Prayer:

_____

Grateful Gift:

_____

Day 2

"Everyone should be quick to listen, slow to speak and slow to become angry." James 1:19

IF ONLY HALF OF THE PEOPLE WALKING THIS planet would abide by James 1:19, we would have a more peaceful and joyful society. I know first-hand that relationships will be saved if we will listen, think and respond with respect. Think of a time with your spouse, children, friend, or family member when you heard a few sentences and then you began with, "I would ... when this happened to me ... you should ... you better. . ."

Now, think of that same situation. How would the ending have looked if you had settled your gaze on the other person, and put away any distractions? What about if you said, "Tell me more"?

_____

_____

_____

_____

_____

Prayer:

_____

Grateful Gift:

_____

Day 3

"He who answers before listening that is his folly and his shame." Proverbs 18:13

THERE ARE SEVERAL BASIC TIPS FOR BEING A BEtter listener. Today, BE fully in the moment with every person with whom you interact. Pick up on key points they are saying and the words they use. Refrain from telling them what to do unless they ask. Only when they ask do you put together a thoughtful reply that is about them and not you. It is okay to say, "Can we get back together and discuss this later?" Or you could say, "May I think about this and get back to you?" Reflect on these conversations and comment below on how you felt.

_____

_____

_____

_____

_____

_____

_____

Prayer:

_____

Grateful Gift:

_____

Day 4

"A fool finds no pleasure in understanding but delights in airing his own opinions." Proverbs 18:2

HOW OFTEN HAVE I BEEN A FOOL? I HAVE MISSED out on so many opportunities to build a strong relationship with someone and to learn more about them. I have to turn my brain on overdrive to keep my mouth shut. We were given two ears and one mouth for a reason. Empathic listening—also called "active listening" or "reflective listening"—is a way of listening and responding to another person that improves mutual understanding and trust. Here is how it works:

1. You pay attention.
2. You do *not* interrupt or provide solutions.
3. You show interest through body language and looking the speaker in the *eye.*
4. You ask questions.
5. You respond appropriately.

Write down the details of a conversation of how you were an active listener today. Did you voice your opinion before you were asked? How did you control your urge to interrupt or offer solutions?

_____

_____

_____

_____

Prayer:

_____

Grateful Gift:

_____

DAY 5

DESCRIBE THE PEOPLE IN YOUR LIFE THAT ARE terrific listeners? What are their skills. How do you feel when you talk to them?

_____

_____

_____

_____

_____

_____

_____

_____

_____

_____

_____

_____

_____

Prayer:

_____

Grateful Gift:

_____

BE Mannerly

Say "please" and "thank you"!

What happened to basic courtesy and mannerly behavior? While I believe every person should read Emily Post's *Etiquette*, I am a realist and we should be aware of the similarities and differences between manners and etiquette. I am talking about manners. Etiquette is connected to protocols and rules and can vary in different cultures and can be modified. Manners are about respect and kindness and should be as universal as a smile. I struggled with this chapter because people are raised differently and have different beliefs. The greatest commandment God gave us was first to love and serve Him, and second, do unto others as we would have them do unto us. Manners show our thoughts and actions and opinions. They reflect who we are and what we believe.

My daughters will likely tell you, I have unrealistic rules and expectations. Sitting up straight and walking with your head high, looking people in the eye, and being polite is nonnegotiable. You can fart at the dinner table, but you better not grunt when asked a question and you better say "please" and "thank you."

There are twelve basic manners that I believe if we lived every day, there would be more smiles, less rage, and people would be happier. Manners are truly about kindness and respect. How does this relate to happiness and being a better person?

1. Say "Please", "Thank you", "Excuse me", and "Bless you." Also, "yes" and "no", not "yeah" and "ugh."
2. RSVP when you receive an invitation.
3. Write a thank you note.
4. Do not put the phone on the table during meals or in meetings. Basically, if someone is around, leave the phone out of sight unless, of course, you are waiting for an important call. Let the important person across from you know the situation.
5. When someone lets you in front of them in traffic, wave a thank you and throw a smile.
6. Be on time. If you're early, you're on time. If you're on time, you're late.
7. Your animals are adorable, but they don't need to go everywhere with you and they certainly don't need to jump or sniff another's crotch.
8. If you are to stand easier than an elderly person or someone holding a child, allow them to sit.
9. Look people in the eye.
10. Do not talk with food in your mouth.
11. Know when to call and when to text. There are certain things worth calling instead of a text. Be thoughtful.
12. Leave things better than you found them.

Day 1

"Still other seed fell on good soil. It came up, grew and produced a crop multiplying thirty, sixty, even a hundred times." Mark 4:8

READ MARK 4:1-20. THESE VERSES CAPTURE the parable of the sower. Look at the list of twelve above, and comment on how you can sow a stronger crop through respect and manners. Pick at least two that you are consistent about doing. Pick at least two that might need some work. Why are you good at some and not the others?

_____

_____

_____

_____

_____

_____

_____

_____

_____

Prayer:

_____

Grateful Gift:

_____

DAY 2

"Love one another with brotherly affection. Outdo one another in showing honor." Romans 12:10

WE CAN SHOW HONOR AND LOVE TO ONE another by looking at them in the eye. The eye is the window to the soul. When you look people in the eye, it shows respect, appreciation, interest, and lets the other person know they are valuable. Think of every situation you encounter face to face. How do you feel when someone looks around you?

_____

_____

_____

_____

_____

_____

_____

_____

Prayer:

_____

Grateful Gift:

_____

Day 3

Look back at the list of twelve basic manners. What else needs to be on this list? As you write them below, comment on why it's important and how you practice it.

_____

_____

_____

_____

_____

_____

_____

_____

_____

_____

_____

_____

_____

Prayer

_____

Grateful Gift:

_____

Day 4

"To speak evil of no one, to avoid quarreling, to be gentle, and to show perfect courtesy toward all people." Titus 3:2

I HAVE SEEN SOME OF THE WORST BEHAVIOR OF human nature at the airport and on planes. For those that choose the airplane for travel, your patience has likely been tested. Taking your shoes and belt off, forgetting that peanut butter is a liquid, and that quarter-ounce of water you didn't drink will cause you to lose the whole bottle. You make it to the gate and your plane is delayed two hours. . . three hours. . . four hours. The secret is out: the airline staff want to be home or to your destination as much as you do. That mother trying to quiet the squealing child whose ears feel like they will explode, wants him to be quiet and pain-free more than you do. The man that just fell asleep snoring on your shoulder is not your husband. And just when you dozed off, "What can I get you to drink?" Who will you BE at this moment? You can BE the bright spot in someone's day. Think of a time when you could have behaved more mannerly and describe how you responded. How could you have made the entire situation better by following some basic manners?

_____

_____

_____

_____

_____

_____

_____

_____

_____

_____

_____

_____

Prayer:

_____

Grateful Gift:

_____

Day 5

"You are the light of the world. A town built on a hill cannot be hidden." Matthew 5:14

BE THE LIGHT. IT IS DIFFICULT TO BE DIFFERENT and stand out from the crowd. You are the town that cannot be hidden. When you offer yourself to others with your time and talents, you stand out. Your light can shine in the simplest of ways. You could RSVP to a party on time and before the host has to remind you. You could take a hostess gift to a gathering. Where is there darkness today? How can you offer your light?

_____

_____

_____

_____

_____

_____

_____

Prayer:

_____

Grateful Gift:

_____

WEEK 3

BE GENEROUS

"We make a living by what we get, we make a life by what we give." Winston Churchill

BEING GENEROUS WITH YOUR TIME, TALENTS, and treasures can take many forms. BEing generous does not just mean with your financial treasures. Sure, money might help the young single mom, but she might also need your help finding a job or maybe you could watch her child one night while she exercises or just spends time by herself. Generosity of your time might include picking up some additional grocery items for a neighbor or the food pantry.

We make tough decisions about giving and our family tries to stay focused. For the first ten birthday parties, both daughters forfeited gifts and instead collected items for their favorite causes. They collected peanut butter for the local food pantry, pet food and towels for the animal shelter, and underwear, socks, teen clothes, and accessories for PACE Center for Girls. To this day, they donate a portion of their work pay or allowance to church or a charity. They created a movement among their peers and for that, I am eternally proud. Your genuine generosity reflects your values.

Day 1

"One man gives freely, yet gains even more, another
withholds unduly but comes to poverty. A generous
man will prosper, he who refreshes others will himself
be refreshed." Proverbs 11:24-25

ADAM RIFKIN WAS LISTED BY *FORTUNE* AS THE
best networker, and at the time, had more LinkedIn connections than any other. Rifkin is a giver, as described by
Adam Grant in his book, *Give and Take: A Revolutionary
Approach to Success.* Rifkin coined "the five-minute favor." Its
premise is you can help anyone in five minutes. Some ideas
include connecting someone looking for a job to someone
who might help or reading and commenting on a resume.
What are some five-minute favors you can do today?

_____

_____

_____

_____

_____

_____

_____

_____

_____

_____

BE 12

Prayer:

_____

Grateful Gift:

_____

Day 2

Jesus looked up and saw the rich putting their gifts into the offering box, and he saw a poor widow put in two small copper coins. And he said, "Truly, I tell you, this poor widow has put in more than all of them. For they all contributed out of their abundance, but she out of her poverty put in all she had to live on." Luke 21:1-4

THIS PASSAGE CAME TO LIFE FOR ME DURING the time Sean cared for his mom. As I shared in BEing Faithful, there were days I didn't know how we would pay the mortgage. Looking back, I still am not sure how we paid all our bills. I was so blessed with stable clients and our cutting back on luxuries was a lesson that led me to a more valuable life. During this period of time, we never stopped giving to our church or to those who were in need. God always provided.

Describe a tough financial time when you doubted if God would provide, and share how He answered your prayers.

_____

_____

_____

_____

_____

_____

_____

Prayer:

_____

Grateful Gift:

_____

Day 3

"Only a life lived for others is a life worthwhile."
Albert Einstein

I BELIEVE IN THE VALUE OF A COMMUNITY. A community will give back to you what you put in it. I have met marvelous people through community outreach and engagement. God calls us to be part of His community.

What does your community look like? Whether work, church, friends, or civic community, how are you generous with your time and talents in your community? What areas could you be more engaged?

_____

_____

_____

_____

_____

_____

_____

_____

Prayer:

_____

Grateful Gift:

_____

Day 4

The point is this: whoever sows sparingly will also reap sparingly, and whoever sows bountifully will also reap bountifully. Each one must give as he has decided in his heart, not reluctantly or under compulsion, for God loves a cheerful giver. And God is able to make all grace abound to you so that having all sufficiency in all things at all times, you may abound in every good work. 2 Corinthians 9:6-8

GOD IS SO GOOD. HE DOES NOT MINCE WORDS. Sow and reap are mentioned numerous times in the Bible to illustrate how our actions can yield rewards. Think about your harvest and what you have sown AND reaped. What do you cultivate? A spirit of love, generosity, and kindness, or are you sowing discourse and judgment? What do you reap from each?

_____

Prayer:

_____

Grateful Gift:

_____

DAY 5

"But if anyone has the world's goods and sees his brother in need, yet closes his heart against him, how does God's love abide in him?" 1 John 3:17

WE MAY NOT REALIZE THE ABUNDANT BLESS-ings we have. We have many goods that aren't financial. Look around you for those in need today. What causes are you passionate about and how can your generosity help? Is it the local animal shelter, hospital, homeless shelter, or something else? It might be a family member or friend who just needs a quick call or word of encouragement. Look around at your office. Do you see suffering where you can bring joy?

_____

_____

_____

_____

_____

_____

_____

Prayer:

_____

Grateful Gift:

_____

RESPECT

TO GET IT, YOU MUST GIVE IT. THE HEBREW word for respect is 'kavod' which means heavy or give extra weight. When we respect others we are treating them with extra attention. Teaching respect to our teenage daughters is a parenting dilemma. Megan and Molly are mannerly, kind, and generous. I struggled to explain respect while making sure they found their voice and advocated for themselves. At times, they would criticize teachers and their styles. I struggled with being too parental and judgmental while trying to explain that people and position deserve our respect. The most valuable lesson I learned was to be the role model for respect.

This scenario applies to many situations and disrespect is usually a result of our need to BE seen, recognized or heard. I created a respect acronym to help me abide in this value.

RESPECT: find out what it means to me:

Recognize
Eye to Eye
Smile
Praise
Engage
Considerate
Time

Review traits of respectful people and see how these fit with the RESPECT acronym:

- RECOGNIZE others
- make EYE TO EYE contact
- SMILE – others will feel valued and you will feel BEtter
- PRAISE – a genuine compliment is respectful
- ENGAGE – learn about others, listen and ask questions
- be CONSIDERATE
- take the TIME to connect with others

This week put the traits and RESPECT acronym into play.

Day 1

Recognize the relationship is important.

Think of an interaction where you can either be respectful or not. It can be as small as saying "hello" to those you pass on the street, in the office, or the grocery store. Or perhaps take the high road when you're having a crucial conversation. Describe interactions where you have recognized that respecting someone else was more important than BEing selfish.

_____

_____

_____

_____

_____

_____

_____

_____

_____

_____

_____

_____

_____

_____

_____

Day 2

Make eye contact and smile.

Numerous studies have shown that people who make eye contact with others are perceived as being more; powerful, warm, likeable, qualified, trustworthy, sincere, and confident. Smiling boosts your immune system because your whole body relaxes when you smile. Smiles are contagious. Body language and mood are linked. Today, make a conscious effort to look at people directly in the eye and smile at everyone you encounter. Try it! Now, record how you felt and count the people that smiled back.

_____

_____

_____

_____

_____

_____

_____

_____

_____

_____

_____

_____

_____

_____

Day 3

Praise others.

Compliments are healing in many ways. They take the focus off of you. Just like when we are being respectful, we are asking ourselves, how does she feel? Compliments spark creativity. We learned several months ago about the value of BEing creative. Be honest and genuine and remember: what goes around comes around. List some compliments you have given and ones that you have received.

_____

_____

_____

_____

_____

_____

_____

_____

_____

_____

_____

_____

_____

_____

DAY 4

Engage and BE considerate.

The word "engage" speaks for itself: to attract and involve. BEing respectful includes capturing the other person's values and BEing considerate of their position. Too often, my opinions cause me to crash as I am merging onto the high road.

What prevents you from showing respect?

_____

_____

_____

_____

_____

_____

_____

_____

_____

_____

_____

_____

_____

_____

_____

_____

_____

_____

Day 5

Take time to treat others as you want to be treated.

It is called the "Golden Rule" for a reason. Matthew 7:12 reminds us to treat others as we want to be treated. It takes time to slow your mind and motion to focus on others. Being respectful takes time, so in every interaction today, ask yourself, "How do I want to be treated?" and watch the change occur. Describe how you live the 'golden rule'.

_____

_____

_____

_____

_____

_____

_____

_____

_____

_____

_____

_____

_____

_____

_____

_____

BE TRANSFORMATIVE

Remember The Blinker

BE Transformative

"Do not conform to the pattern of this world but be transformed by the renewing of your mind. Then you will be able to test and approve what God's will is— his good, pleasing and perfect will." Romans 12:2

Having been filled with BE 12 energy, I hope you have created a "new normal." As you throw out the old and focus on the new, here are some tips to navigate your road to "new normal." May your lane be filled with strength and faith when things change. May you seek wisdom as you drive at any speed. May you keep your groove, even if you sway off the road. May you be brave and slowly get back in the lane when you hear the obnoxious shoulder scream. You know, the sound your tires make when you veer onto the shoulder. And may you 'turn on your blinker' before you merge into another's lane.

"And I am certain that God, who began a good work within you, will continue his work until it is finally finished on the day when Christ Jesus returns." Philippians 1:6

Read Proverbs 31:10-31. The Proverbs 31 woman was a significant foundation for this book. Twelve messages ring loud from the Proverbs 31 woman. In the blank beside each trait, describe how you exhibit it.

1. Noble character is of utmost value: _____

_____

_____

_____

2. Willingly works hard: _____

_____

_____

_____

3. Makes sure her family and those important to her are fed: _____

_____

_____

_____

4. Businesswoman who seeks opportunity: _____

_____

_____

_____

5. She cares for others, making sure they are clothed: _____

_____

_____

_____

6. She invests well: _____

_____

_____

_____

7. She is strong: _____

_____

_____

_____

8. She takes care of the needy: _____

_____

_____

_____

9. She has strength and dignity: _____

_____

_____

_____

10. She does not worry about the future: _____

_____

_____

_____

11. She speaks with wisdom: _____

_____

_____

_____

12. Faith resonates from her mouth: _____

_____

_____

_____

BE an advocate, prayerful and passionate.

Week 1

BE an Advocate

"Never doubt that a small group of thoughtful, committed citizens can change the world; indeed, it's the only thing that ever has." Margaret Mead

Gal pals, we need to be the change! Advocacy has existed for centuries in many forms and it is never more needed than now. The Oxford English Dictionary dates "advocacy" as a noun first appearing in the 1300s. *Advocateus* means to be called or summoned, especially to be called to one's aid. This is not political, it is principled. We need to be educated and engaged and not harmful and heartless.

Advocacy has been my life and career. Dating back to when I was a young girl, my father was a passionate advocate. He served at senior living facilities. He was a "Big" with Big Brothers, Big Sisters and taught at-risk men to fish and took them to church. So, when God delivered me to the realm of lobbying, I put my advocacy service to work. For twenty years, I have had a meaningful lobbying career. I have written legislation, obtained millions of dollars in funding for children's healthcare and the most vulnerable citizens, and been a part of major policy change. I was involved in obtaining money for abused children; wrote legislation to fund trauma centers, ill children, and research centers; and crafted policy for jobs, education, and healthcare. The successes came because people believed in me and provided guidance and mentoring. Some things cannot be learned in school or from reading, but by observing and asking. I have a long list of mentors, elected officials, and leaders that I deeply thank for teaching me the value of a great advocate. You can be the CHANGE you want to see in the system.

The political chaos and unrest rocked our nation for years in the mid to late 2000s. Yet, women across the nation rose to the task with a record number of us serving in Congress in 2019. BE educated about the candidates, policy and BE engaged.

You are likely already an advocate in that you "advocate" for your kids, your employees, a cause dear to your heart, or an issue. You can speak for someone whose voice cannot be heard. This week, we will explore advocating for ourselves and others.

DAY 1

"But let justice roll on like a river, righteousness like a never-failing stream." Amos 5:24

WHAT BREAKS YOUR HEART? FOR AS LONG AS you need, think of an issue, problem, or situation that breaks your heart. Is it hunger, abuse, homelessness, water quality? What causes you to pause each time this issue comes forward? What skills can you bring to the issue? Inform, educate, and engage in the cause that breaks your heart. Could you take clothes to an abuse shelter? Furniture, sheets, and towels are always needed as the homeless move to transitional living.

_____

_____

_____

_____

_____

_____

_____

Prayer:

_____

Grateful Gift:

_____

Day 2

*"Speak up for those who cannot speak for themselves,
for the rights of all who are destitute. Speak up and
judge fairly; defend the rights of the poor and needy."*
Proverbs 31:8-9

WHILE THERE STILL MAY BE CONSTRAINTS,
voting is a freedom for women in every country except
Vatican City. However, let it be known: some men cannot
vote there, either. A 2017 CAWP Rutgers report showed
voter turnout rates for women have equaled or exceeded
those for men. In 2016, 63.3% of eligible women voted.
Women changed the outcome of the 2018 midterm elec-
tions. After a record number of female candidates on bal-
lots across the country, more women now serve in the US
House and US Senate than ever before.

If you aren't already a registered voter, please register to
vote and *vote*. Most US states offer a mail-in ballot or early
voting. Know your local elected officials and their values.
Who is your mayor or county/city commissioner? Who
is your state Legislator both in the state House and state
Senate? Who is your Congressman? Who is your Senator?
Read about at least some of them to find out where they
stand on issues.

Above all, vote! Can you tell I am passionate about this?
We live in a free country and I would remind you, if you do
not vote, you do not have the "freedom" to complain about
the situation. If something or someone angers you, act with
your voice. When is your next election?

_____

_____

_____

_____

_____

_____

_____

_____

_____

_____

_____

_____

_____

_____

_____

_____

Prayer:

_____

Grateful Gift:

_____

Day 3

"Ask, and it will be given to you seek, and you will find;
knock, and it will be opened to you." Matthew 7:7

ADVOCATE FOR YOURSELF. ASK FOR THE PRO-
motion, the additional responsibilities, stand your ground
for something you believe, and speak up in a loving way to
make your position heard. Describe a time you have advocated for yourself and the strength it gave you.

_____

_____

_____

_____

_____

_____

_____

_____

_____

_____

Prayer:

_____

Grateful Gift:

_____

Day 4

"This is what the Lord Almighty said: 'Administer true justice; show mercy and compassion to one another." Zechariah 7:9

DAILY, WE ARE GIVEN THE OPPORTUNITY TO show justice, mercy, and compassion. People poor in spirit are all around you. A few days ago, you shared what broke your heart. What organization is helping the cause? Who are the people impacted and how can you show mercy? If you are already volunteering, write down how you are showing compassion for these people.

_____

_____

_____

_____

_____

_____

_____

_____

Prayer:

_____

Grateful Gift:

_____

Day 5

TODAY, I URGE YOU TO PUT ADVOCACY IN ACTION. You have identified what breaks your heart and how you are helping. Today, write an email or letter to a decision-maker or elected official that can do something to help. If you don't know what policy change needs to occur, call the organization and ask them. It is likely that your state elected official may have some impact. For example, United Way is focused on financial stability and early learning. Are there policies that limit programs that serve these populations?

_____

_____

_____

_____

_____

_____

_____

_____

Prayer:

_____

Grateful Gift:

_____

BE Prayerful

"Do not be anxious about anything, but in everything by prayer and supplication with thanksgiving let your requests be made known to God. And the peace of God, which surpasses all understanding, will guard your hearts and your minds in Christ Jesus."
Philippians 4:6-7

I KNOW THE POWER OF PRAYER. WE HAVE A prayer basket on our kitchen table. It is full of requests from a dying friend to swim goals to trusting God will help us BE better friends and citizens. God has healed a swimmer's hurt shoulder, blessed me with the right words for a hard conversation, and lifted many a heavy heart. As someone who likes feeling in control, prayer is one thing I **can** do to help others. I pray everywhere. I pray while swimming laps in the pool, running along the beach, in the car, and fall to my knees to the Lord's Prayer. I stop, drop, and pray everywhere. Read Psalm 23 now and let it digest and you dissect its call.

For me, a prayerful life includes a daily reflection in the books of Psalms and Proverbs. I start each year with Psalm 1 and Proverbs 1 and read a chapter a day, then repeat. The joy, anguish, and supplication in Psalms always comes at the right time. The wisdom in Proverbs guides me through adoration and confession.

DAY 1

"And above all, pray." Ephesians 6:10

I FOUND PRAYING "ACTS" IS A GOOD METHOD.
I learned this acronym early in my walk with God:
Adoration, Confession, Thanksgiving, and Supplication
(ACTS). Following this pattern helps us focus on submitting to God. Today, write down your prayers.

Adoration

_____

_____

_____

Confession

_____

_____

_____

Thanksgiving

_____

_____

_____

Supplication

_____

_____

_____

Day 2

"Therefore, I tell you, whatever you ask in prayer,
believe that you have received it, and it will be yours."
Mark 11:24

MANY OF US HAVE DIFFICULTY UNDERSTANDING these verses. Since God knows the plans He has for us, He may not give us that new job or car we think we deserve. What He will give us is exactly what we need when we need it.

The miracles I have seen from God's wonderous hands are the results not only of his love but of constant prayer. Fasting is one activity that has helped my prayer life. Fasting is present in many forms and I encourage you to explore it as a tool in your belt. Look back at the prayers you have written in this book. Describe the outcomes below. What did your prayer life look like before you started BEing! How do you value prayer? Do you throw a few words on paper or do you dig deep to fully experience the benefits? Is your faithful value strong enough to know God is in control? Share your heart as you answer these questions.

_____

_____

_____

_____

_____

_____

Prayer:

_____

Grateful Gift:

_____

Day 3

"Devote yourselves to prayer, being watchful and thankful." Colossians 4:2

DESCRIBE YOUR PRAYER LIFE. WHEN DO YOU pray? For what and then what? Do you Believe God will answer your prayers according to His purpose? How are you watching and waiting for God to answer, and then, how do you thank Him?

_____

_____

_____

_____

_____

_____

_____

_____

_____

_____

Prayer:

_____

Grateful Gift:

_____

DAY 4

"Be joyful in hope, patient in affliction, faithful in prayer." Romans 12:12

ONE OF MY BEST GAL PALS, JULES, IS SOLID IN her faith and teaches me so much about walking with God. She has been through turmoil, tragedy, and through deep valleys. We lobbied the halls of Tallahassee together for over ten years. We were pregnant together, have picked each other up from being publicly yelled at by a senator, and survived failures together. Her son, Fisher, had a brain tumor and I watched the deepest faith and dedication I have ever seen. She never stopped praying. She was a walking example of joy, hope, patience, affliction, and above all, faith. Our prayer warriors gathered on calls to pray with her before, during, and after the surgery. We continued to pray and gather online or on the phone. After months and much agony for her entire family, God continued to deliver miracles. Fisher celebrated a year of being free from cancer. God is great.

I know your faith has been tested. Describe the situation. How did God deliver you? What tips did you employ or Bible verses you focused on that carried you through?

_____

_____

_____

BE 12

Prayer:

_____

Grateful Gift:

_____

DAY 5

"Call to me and I will answer you and tell you great and unsearchable things you do not know." Jeremiah 33:3

DURING MY "LOST YEAR," I RAN OVER THIRTY miles a week. Running helps me cope. It is my prayer time. I pray with every step I take. I pray for people, peace, grace, and answers. During this tough time, I prayed for answers. At least three days a week, I ran at five in the morning. There were mornings that I don't know how I made it back to my door. My mind was clouded with negative and self-doubting thoughts. My esteem was at its lowest. I am blessed to run on beautiful tree-lined streets of St. Petersburg and along the dolphin-filled Tampa Bay. I see families, bikers, walkers, people roller blading and pushing strollers. There was one man who lit a burning bush for me. I saw him every morning in his wheelchair with his dog. Then, one morning, I felt the hand of God like I had not before. I smiled at this man. The next day, I smiled at twelve people. Nine of the twelve smiled back. Then, number ten was the man in the wheelchair. He smiled back and said, "Thank you for smiling."

The next day, I saw a couple walking hand in hand, I smiled and said, "You look happy."

They both smiled and said, "We are."

I continued this pattern and every day I felt lighter and lighter. My biggest regret is that I never stopped to get to know and subsequently thank the man in the wheelchair.

BE prayerful and wait for Him to answer. When was the last time you called to God in prayer for answers and direction? Did you pray and believe He would answer as He tells us in the book of Jeremiah?

_____

_____

_____

_____

_____

_____

_____

_____

_____

_____

_____

_____

_____

_____

Prayer:

_____

Grateful Gift:

_____

Week 3

BE Passionate

"Never let loving devotion or faithfulness leave you; bind them around your neck, write them on the tablet of your heart." Proverbs 3:3

I am passionate about the cross. I wear a cross every day. It's either around my neck or on my wrist, my finger, or on a shirt. It reminds me of God's love and faithfulness. Where I fall short is making sure my love for God is seen by others through my actions. I hope the daily Scriptures you have been reading are engraved on your heart.

Earlier this year, you wrote your purpose statement. Read your purpose statement. Hopefully you are reading it regularly. Are you passionate about your purpose? Combining your gifts and talents with your passion can lead to making a significant impact.

The most common adjective people use to describe me is "passionate." I am proud of that, yet it has taken many years and God's grace for me to put that passion to purpose.

Day 1

"And a time to. . ."

WE CONTINUE OUR JOURNEY BUILDING OUR life which is centered on God. The author of the Old Testament book Ecclesiastes "chased after the wind" (1:14). It appears the author's life is largely behind him as he pursued one thing after another, seeking happiness.

Open your Bible and read Ecclesiastes 3:1-12. Select one of the "a time to. . ." from this chapter, and write about your experience. During this time, how did you stay passionate about purpose?

_____

_____

_____

_____

_____

_____

_____

_____

Prayer:

_____

Grateful Gift:

_____

Day 2

Passion put in action is purpose.

WRITE DOWN YOUR PASSIONS, AND DESCRIBE how they are married with purpose. Do your passions include:

- Sharing God's Word?
- Working with children?
- Speaking in front of people?
- Working alone or with people? Inside? Outside?
- What freedoms are important? What "benefits" do you want from this passion?

_____

_____

_____

_____

_____

_____

_____

Prayer:

_____

Grateful Gift:

_____

Day 3

"Keep your mouth free of perversity; keep corrupt talk far from your lips." Proverbs 4:24

THERE ARE SEVERAL WORDS THAT ARE TABOO in our home. Profanity, "stupid", and "I don't care" are not allowed. When you don't stand for something, you fall for everything. Write about what you stand for. What sayings are taboo for you and why? What words do you use to show passion and purpose?

_____

_____

_____

_____

_____

_____

_____

_____

_____

_____

Prayer:

_____

Grateful Gift:

_____

Day 4

"Your word is a lamp for my feet, a light on my path."
Psalm 119:105

I HAVE STRUGGLED WITH BEING PATIENT AND trusting that God will provide as I pursue my passion to serve.

A few days ago, you listed your passions. If you are struggling to put them into purpose, write down action items. God put you here today, and His timing is perfect. Think about when you wake up at night and stumble to the bathroom or kitchen. You need a light for your path. What actions serve as lights to brighten your path and not trip but instead BE on purpose.

_____

_____

_____

_____

_____

_____

_____

Prayer:

_____

Grateful Gift:

_____

DAY 5

"The promise of skillful living is made to all those
how will listen to advice and accept instruction."
Proverbs 19:20

A LITTLE MONDAY MORNING QUARTER-
backing is okay. We can learn when we look back at the
tapes, and see what we could have done better.

Where I have to catch myself is when I let the things I
didn't do drag me into depression. Over the years, I have
had many aspirations of "greatness." Then I realized God
has the playbook if I will listen to His instruction.

How did God speak to you this week about your passion and His purpose?

_____

_____

_____

_____

_____

_____

_____

Prayer:

_____

Grateful Gift:

_____

Week 4

Realize Your Lane

I HAVE LEARNED A LOT ABOUT LANES AND EVEN more about how I can navigate them BEtter. The swim lane has given clarity to how I can BE my BEst. Swimming has been part of my life since I was a "tadpole" at the Frankfort YMCA. Our family is blessed that our daughters are dedicated, competitive swimmers. I believe it is the most challenging sport, and normally, just like at our daughter's high school, the swim team has the highest GPA. Smart and gritty, they are. The pride I have for Megan and Molly is unmatched. Swimming has given them confidence, perseverance, allowed them to achieve their personal best and yet been part of a team.

At the bottom of each of swim lane is a thick black line and a *cross* at the end of each line. The black line has been a focal point for prayer as I see God in the cross each time I finish a lap. During this focused prayer time, I hear God speaking within the soothing calm of gliding through the water. With each breath, I feel grateful for his love and forgiveness.

Sometimes, I am distracted by the swimmer in the lane beside me. In most situations, they are faster than me. My competitive nature sets in and I try to catch up. And it's not pretty. My stroke gets sloppy, the chicken wing comes out,

I get winded, and my flip-turn looks like a seal diving for a fish. By staying in my lane and focusing on *my* swim, I get stronger and BEtter. It requires me to refocus and realize my skills and if I want to BE BEtter, do the work to get there.

Day 1

"They shall mount up with wings like eagles; they shall run and not be weary; they shall walk and not faint."
Isaiah 40:31

Describe a time that you steered into someone else's lane. What prompted you to cross the line without the blinker? Did you think you were smarter like I did? Did you want their skills and not your own? I did. Did you put on the fixer cape and swoop in because you could do it better? I thought so. Have you soared like the eagle and asked for forgiveness? It's never too late. I know.

_____

_____

_____

Day 2

"Therefore, confess your sins to each other and pray for each other so that you may be healed. The prayer of a righteous person is powerful and effective." James 5:16

Think about the times you changed lanes. Whom did you impact? Was it a crash? Did you turn on the blinker? Were

words and actions said that need to be healed? Describe it
below and pray for healing..

Day 3

> *"But when you ask, you must believe and not doubt,*
> *because the one who doubts is like a wave of the sea,*
> *blown and tossed by the wind." James 1:6*

Many waves have crashed over me, and I have been tossed
by the wind. I have doubted my talents and questioned
when God was going to deliver me. I am not a patient
person, but each day I grow to accept His timing and
presence. When I seek God amid the storm, He always
shows up, as there are angels everywhere. Describe when
you have seen and felt His presence. What have you not
doubted that He would deliver?

Day 4

> *"No temptation has overtaken you that is not common*
> *to man. God is faithful, and he will not let you be*
> *tempted beyond your ability, but with the temptation*

he will also provide the way of escape, that you may be
able to endure it." 1 Corinthians 10:13

My virtual Bible study gal pals have been together for almost ten years. We have been through joys, heartache, illness, and death. All of which has led us on a closer walk with God. We have used several verses to keep our focus. Read Joshua 1:9-11, which instructs us not to fear or be dismayed that God will be with us wherever we go. Describe when you have been tempted and how He has helped you "escape." Describe your fear and faith as you endured.

_____

_____

_____

Day 5

"He said to them, 'Because of your little faith. For truly,
I say to you, if you have faith like a grain of mustard
seed, you will say to this mountain, "Move from here
to there," and it will move, and nothing will be impos-
sible for you." Matthew 17:20

I have a mustard seed necklace, and I wear it on days I need a reminder that God can move mountains. Describe a time when God has moved mountains for you.

_____

_____

_____

_____

_____

_____

_____

Stop, Drop, and Pray! And if you haven't read the book by my dear sister in Christ, Barbara Alderfer, please read it.

BE YOURSELF

WHATEVER YOU ARE, BE
A GOOD ONE.

BE Yourself

"In him we were also chosen, having been predestined according to the plan of him who works out everything in conformity with the purpose of his will."
Ephesians 1:11

AT SEVERAL POINTS IN MY LIFE, I HAVE STRUGgled with what purpose God is calling me. As I talked with many gal pals, it is clear many share that yearning and questioning. Often, by comparing ourselves to others and their calling, we lose sight of who we are. One particular morning, I was immobilized by self-doubt, negative talk, and fear that I was a gigantic failure. I knelt and prayed for God to give me direction. I planned to open my Bible, go through the motions, then reach out to gal pals for energy. Instead, my eyes fell to Ephesians 1:11 to remind me God's plan and timing is perfect.

We have spent hours, days, weeks, and months together. Whether you wrestled with your values alone or with friends, I hope you have BEcome your BEst. Living my value system has helped me follow the rules of the road. One is to use the blinker. You've heard my stories of lane changing. There are times to pick a lane, times to stay in your lane, times to slow down and let others pass, and times to speed up and pass. Detours are options on the transformative journey and the most important rules of the road are respect and communication.

Tom Rath's book, *StrengthsFinder 2.0,* which I mentioned earlier, taught me some rules of the road and my "driving" strengths. My top ten strengths are: futuristic, learner, strategic, self-assurance, command, activator, ideation, input, adaptable, and achiever. What this transfers in my personality is an over-functioning fixer who loves to learn and do. Knowing I have command and ideation as my strengths, I know the blinker and other rules of the road are important if I want meaningful relationships. My "old self" barreled into many lanes where I didn't belong. I crashed and hurt people along the way. Fortunately, I learned the power of being humble and apologizing and many forgave me. In all my relationships, I stay focused on my lane and switch lanes only when it is clear and the other "drivers" are welcoming the move.

Character is evident in our actions, words, deeds, and intentions. We develop strong moral character by controlling our thoughts. Read the following verses, and describe how the message in each one speaks to you and your value system.

Philippians 4:8

_____

_____

_____

2 Peter 1:5-6

_____

_____

_____

Proverbs 4:23

_____

_____

_____

Matthew 15:18-20

_____

_____

_____

1 Corinthians 15:33

_____

_____

_____

BE self-aware, mindful, and BrEathe.

Week 1

BE Self-Aware

BEING AWARE OF WHO ARE CAN BE ESPECIALLY hard during conflict and when your confidence is lacking. When you find that friends aren't returning your calls or requests to connect, your boss is ignoring you, or you're not connecting with your spouse or children, do some self-reflecting. The more common response sounds like this: "She is so moody." Or, "My boss is too busy." Perhaps, "My husband would rather watch football." Or, "It's just a phase with my daughter."

While these may have some truths, be truthful with yourself. Now, think about these relationships and the energy and strengths you have given to each. My self-reflection period was the greatest when I left a large, nationally recognized organization, and many people didn't return my calls for coffee. While I recognize now that many of those relationships were transactional, I thought, in many cases, they enjoyed spending time with me and found me an important peer. After reflecting, I came to terms with my skills and what I brought to the table. I BEcame more self-aware and adjusted my actions to best meet the relationships. Most importantly, I realized I needed to let go of those individuals that just did not like me. It is real and it is okay. The wounds will heal as you seek God's love.

Day 1

"Therefore, do not let anyone judge you by what you eat or drink." Colossians 2:16

KNOW THYSELF. EASIER SAID THAN DONE. THIS week dig deep into BEing you. Write down five of your favorite books, five books that you want to read each year, five of your favorite authors, your favorite color, your favorite city and country, your favorite poem, your favorite Disney character, and more. Have fun and get to know how cool you are.

Prayer:

Grateful Gift:

Day 2

*"Am I now trying to win the approval of human beings,
or of God? Or am I trying to please people? If I were
still trying to please people, I would not be a servant
of Christ." Galatians 1:10*

BEING SELF-AWARE IS THE ABILITY TO UNDER-
stand your decisions and being conscious of your actions
and behavior. Our daughter, Molly, possesses this charac-
teristic. We first knew she had a keen sense of who she was
when she was not quite three years old. She came in the
kitchen and said, "I think I need to put myself in time-out."
She had the sense she was going to do something that maybe
she should not.

Name some situations where you were truly conscious
of your actions and how it would impact a situation.

_____

_____

_____

_____

_____

Prayer:

_____

Grateful Gift:

_____

DAY 3

"Whoever walks with the wise becomes wise, but the companion of fools will suffer harm." Proverbs 13:20

MANY FACTORS CAN WREAK HAVOC ON OUR self-awareness. Our pasts, our upbringing, the media, and even our friends. *Show me your friends, and I'll show you your future.* Right relationships are the key not only to success, but to staying on track with our God-given destiny. The relationships that we nurture either distract us from our calling or launch us toward His plan for our lives.

Describe your friends by name and what they do to bring out the best in you. Write down their qualities and values. If you haven't told them how much they mean to you, take a minute and do it.

_____

_____

_____

_____

_____

_____

Prayer:

_____

Grateful Gift:

_____

Day 4

*"For you **created** my inmost being; you knit me together in my mother's womb. I praise you because I am fearfully and wonderfully made; your works are wonderful, I know that full well." Psalm 139:13-14*

WE WERE CREATED BY GOD FOR A PURPOSE. IT is so easy to compare our bodies, our personalities, and our skills to others. Let us praise Him for our strengths. Write down your strengths and your skills. Years ago, a mentor urged me to create a "sunshine file" filled with my accomplishments, lessons learned, and reminders of the good work I did. She also reminded me to keep my resume current, which I do every six to eight months. What is in your sunshine file?

_____

_____

_____

_____

_____

_____

Prayer:

_____

Grateful Gift:

_____

Day 5

*"For we are God's handiwork, created in Christ Jesus
to do good works, which God prepared in advance for
us to do." Ephesians 2:10*

GOD CREATED US TO DO GOOD WITHOUT
blaming or complaining. Are you either of these?
Complainer literally means "one who is discontented with
his lot in life. It is akin to the word "grumbler." Complaining
is certainly not a fruit of the Spirit. In fact, it is detrimental
to the peace, joy, and patience that come from the Spirit.
For the Christian, complaining is destructive. It only serves
to make our witness to the world more difficult. Negative
thoughts are unhealthy. Most oncologists will tell you their
first bit of advice to a newly diagnosed cancer patient it to
remove any negative parts or people in your life.

Are you a blamer? Do you look for excuses when you
make a mistake or fall short of a meeting a goal or a dead-
line? Or when you forget to do something?

*"A good name is more desirable than great riches; to be
esteemed is better than silver or gold." Proverbs 22:1*

What do people think of you? Are you aware of your brand?
Building and maintaining your brand is hard. Between my
lost year, caring for my mother, and my "spell", I wasn't sure
who I was and if I was good at much. I felt deserted by
people I thought were friends. But what started to happen
when I let God take control is that I BEcame at peace with

myself. The self-reflection that I have led you through in this book was healing for me. God has already prepared the good works I will do.

What is your brand? Describe how you see yourself. Today, ask two or three friends or family to describe you.

I must tell you, this will be hard on others. I tried this and plenty of people didn't want to be honest with me. Keep scanning your village until you find an honest person that cares enough about you to give feedback.

_____

_____

_____

_____

_____

_____

_____

_____

_____

_____

Prayer:

_____

Grateful Gift:

_____

BE Mindful

"All the unhappiness of men arises from one simple fact: that they cannot sit quietly in their chamber." Blaise Pascal, 17ᵗʰ Century French mathematician

MUCH HAS BEEN WRITTEN THE LAST TEN years about mindfulness and meditation and its power on the brain. It is a practice of focusing on the moment and examining your thoughts and emotions. Studies have found that meditation can help ease psychological stresses like anxiety, depression, and pain. A Harvard study found that mindful relaxation such as meditation improves health. Over a period of eight weeks, the control group practiced mindfulness exercises for an average of twenty-seven minutes a day. The results of MRI scans found increased gray-matter density in the hippocampus, known to be important for learning and memory, and in structures associated with self-awareness, compassion, and introspection.

Mindfulness is maintaining a moment-by-moment awareness of our thoughts, feelings, and our environment. It involves acceptance and paying attention to our feelings without judging them. As I shared earlier, I believe in the power of yoga and I have some dreams about how it can be a Christian ministry for women. Yoga has introduced calm and self-acceptance to me. The awareness it brings me lifts my spirits. Focusing on breathing and clearing the mind is therapy for me as it reduces any stress I am carrying. I urge you to take back your life by grasping the healing value of mindfulness.

Day 1

"Set your mind on things above not on earthly things."
Colossians 3:2

WHEREVER YOU GO, THERE YOU ARE. SO WHY are we allowing the distractions to cloud our moments? One hundred and fifty years ago, the telephone didn't exist. Fifty years ago, the Internet didn't exist, and twenty-five years ago, Google didn't exist. Today, you are challenged to develop a new outlook on your phone and social media engagement. If you are active on Facebook, can you give it up for the day? If you shop online, can you fill that time with another activity? What are your cell phone rules for yourself and your family? If you don't have them, make them. Record what you are going to do in relation to managing social media engagement so you can free the space to be mindful.

_____

_____

_____

_____

_____

Prayer:

_____

Grateful Gift.

_____

Day 2

"Meditate in your heart upon your bed and be still."
Psalm 4:4b

COMMIT TO BOLD MOVES TODAY. TRY TO MED-
itate for five minutes and then build up to ten and more as
you practice. Find a quiet place void of distractions. Put your
phone away. Sit in a comfortable position, usually cross-
legged. Start breathing in through your nostrils without
trying to control your breath. Just breath in and out. At first,
your mind will be cluttered. Bring your focus back to the
breath. After you have finished, you will be more relaxed
and your mind will feel clear. Write any thoughts you had
about the experience.

_____

_____

_____

_____

_____

_____

_____

Prayer:

_____

Grateful Gift:

_____

Day 3

So, do not worry, saying, "What shall we eat" or "What shall we drink" or "What shall we wear." For the pagans run after all these things and your heavenly Father knows that you need them. But seek first his kingdom and his righteousness and all these things will be given to you as well. Therefore, do not worry about tomorrow for tomorrow will worry about itself. Each day has enough trouble of its own. Matthew 6:31-34

As a child, I constantly worried. Sunday nights before school were often filled with tears as I thought about the coming week. My worry and anxiety lessened as I BEcame confident in God's plan for me. Part of that confidence rose from deliberate actions to seek His righteousness. For me, it became finding true friends that brought out the best in me. I finally won the compare game.

I read that the average person has between 50,000-70,000 thoughts per day. No wonder we don't know ourselves. Much of those thoughts are worrying about what others think of us or what others have.

I finally won the jackpot of the compare game. I didn't win it by pumping more quarters to the slots. I started my attitude of gratitude list. I wrote down at least three blessings a day. Are you worried today? Is it overcoming you? It is changing the way you treat yourself and others? Being mindful creates a new sense of calm. Describe how being mindful creates a sense of calm for you.

_____

_____

_____

_____

_____

_____

_____

_____

_____

_____

_____

_____

_____

_____

_____

Prayer:

_____

Grateful Gift:

_____

Day 4

"Let your eyes look straight ahead; fix your gaze directly before you." Proverbs 4:25

MULTI-TASKING IS PASSÉ. WE NOW KNOW damage to the brain and heart along with low productivity result when trying to juggle too many balls. Clifford Nass, a psychology professor at Stanford University, says today's nonstop multitasking wastes more time than it saves. It may be killing our concentration and creativity too.

Watch yourself today. Are you on a conference call while responding to emails? Do you need to stop multi-tasking? What is keeping you on the hamster wheel? Fix your gaze on the one thing you want to accomplish and feel your heart rate slow down.

_____

_____

_____

_____

_____

_____

Prayer:

_____

Grateful Gift:

_____

Day 5

"Be still in the presence of the Lord and wait patiently for him to act." Psalm 37:7

HONOR THE SABBATH. SELECT SATURDAY, Sunday, or another day to be screen, phone, and work free. Can you do it? Reflect how you feel at the end of your Sabbath and BEing mindful in the moment. On one of your Sabbaths, write yourself a letter. Describe where you are, who is around you, and what you are doing. Describe as many details as you can about yourself and your value system. Where has your decision taken you?

_____

_____

_____

_____

_____

_____

_____

_____

Prayer:

_____

Grateful Gift:

_____

WEEK 3

BrEathe

You know what happens when you stop breathing.

Let's explore what happens when we *start* breathing. Over the last few months, we have seen the value of deep breaths before a crucial conversation or when hurtful words are spoken to you. Deep, rhythmic breathing has been proven to manage stress and anxiety, lower blood pressure and heart rate, and boost brain health. Deep breathing may be called diaphragmatic breathing, abdominal breathing, and belly breathing. Visualize and try what I am talking about. When you breathe deeply, air comes in through your nose and fills your lungs, and the lower belly rises.

I found the life-saving value of deep breathing during a long bout with heartache and sadness. There was a period of time that I battled with depression. I knew in the moment that I was the root of my problems but I couldn't get out of my way. I could not catch my breath in yoga, in the pool, at work, or at home. For weeks, I told myself I wasn't good enough at anything, whether work and personal. I let all the negativity fill my heart, head, actions and words. A few things saved me. My dear gal pal Katie reminded me, "Action is the enemy of anxiety." So, while I wanted to lay fetal in my bed, I started making big changes to my lifestyle.

And I started with deep belly breathing. You'll try it this week. I also wrote myself a few letters. I reset my vision and values statement. I am praying that you experience the value of BrEath.

The statistics on anxiety and depression are staggering. Yet, I challenge you to BE the change. Knowing the statistics about mental health and understanding the value of deep breathing can help you BE. Anxiety and depression are real and there are tools for us to use. The National Center for Health Statistics (NCHS) 2011 report found that one in ten Americans take antidepressants. And, twenty-three percent of the women in their 40s and 50s take antidepressants. According to the World Health Organization, depression ranked as the third leading cause of the global burden of disease in 2004 and will move into the first place by 2030. Breathing is the answer to stressful situations and was proven by a Stanford study on post-traumatic stress disorder. The study, conducted with veterans, used yoga and breathing to help PTSD victims heal. And hear this: the Defense Department, the government, because of the study, is advocating breathing techniques be used in therapy.

The healing power of deep, focused breathing is working. The practice has stopped me from saying something I might regret, calmed my racing heart when I "needed an aspirin" and is healing the debilitating condition of tinnitus in a loved one.

Day 1

BREATHE. TODAY, PAUSE FOR TEN MINUTES. FIND a place to sit in silence with a clear mind. Rid the area of pens and paper and be prepared to cleanse your mind. Find a quiet, happy place. Sit or lie down. Take a normal breath. Then try a deep breath to the count of 1..2..3..4..5 Breathe in slowly through your nose, allowing your chest and lower belly to rise as your lungs fill. Let your abdomen expand fully. Now breathe out slowly to the count 5..4..3..2..1. Continue the process of with your eyes closed. Combine your breathing with imagery or a word or phrase that helps you relax and remove those toxins. Describe your success.

_____

_____

_____

_____

_____

_____

_____

Prayer:

_____

Grateful Gift:

_____

Day 2

"Create in me a pure heart, O God, and renew a stead-fast spirit within me." Psalm 51:10

BREATHING PROVIDES A REFRESHED AND renewed spirit. When I know I have a difficult situation in front of me or someone says something that pushes my buttons, I pause and take a few breaths. It calms me and allows for my heart and mind to be more open.

Think about a time that you reacted when someone said a hurtful or stabbing comment. I presume your body tensed. What situation may present itself today that needs your calmness?

_____

_____

_____

_____

_____

_____

_____

Prayer:

_____

Grateful Gift:

_____

Day 3

"Take delight in the Lord, and he will give you the desires of your heart." Psalm 37:4

A FEW WEEKS AGO, WE WROTE OURSELVES A letter. Write yourself another letter, and describe where you will be and what you will be doing in ten years. Describe as many details as you can about yourself and your value system. Where have your decisions taken you?

_____

_____

_____

_____

_____

_____

_____

_____

_____

_____

Prayer:

_____

Grateful Gift:

_____

DAY 4

"Go! It will be done just as you believed it would."
Matthew 8:13

HAVE YOU EVER HAD A LONG DAY WITH DEMANDS after demands, hurt feelings, or just exhaustion? If you have been in the office all day or been in the home preparing for your family, how do you react when you greet them?

Open your Bible to Matthew, Chapter 8 and see how your day compared. Jesus has been at it all day. He came down from a mountain, which, if you hike, you know isn't necessarily easy, after sharing God's Word all day. He healed a man with leprosy, a centurion who was paralyzed, and Peter's mother-in-law. He tries to take a nap in the boat as He and the disciples crossed the lake and a furious storm erupted. He woke and calmed the winds and waves.

We all get tired. What are your waves and winds right now? Is it wanting to control others? Situations you cannot? List them and ask God to equip you to calm the storm. Take some deep breaths and pray that He will guide you in your list and in your weathering the storm.

_____

_____

Prayer:

_____

Grateful Gift:

_____

DAY 5

"Test me, Lord, and try me, examine my heart and my mind." Psalm 26:2

YOU HAVE GIVEN SO MUCH OF YOUR TIME AND reflection to gain a BEtter understanding of your heart and mind. What days were you frustrated and why? God will not test you beyond what you can bear. Acknowledge where you had to stretch and the results.

_____

_____

_____

_____

_____

_____

_____

_____

_____

Prayer:

_____

Grateful Gift:

_____

WEEK 4

REFLECT

So, Jesus took him aside privately, away from the crowd, and put His fingers into the man's ears. Then He spit and touched the man's tongue. And looking up to heaven, He signed deeply and said to him, "Ephphatha!" which means be opened. And immediately the man's ears were opened and his tongue was released, and he began to speak plainly. Mark 7:33-34

Day 1

Ephphatha! Ephphatha! Ephphatha! Say that three times. It means BE open. As we end our time together, I hope you are just BEginning to BE open to the boundless person you have BEcome. Today, look back on your notes throughout the year and write about the one value where you need to BE more open to understanding and BEcoming your BEst.

_____

_____

_____

_____

_____

Day 2

What is the most pertinent Bible verse you found during the last twelve months? Why is it so meaningful to you? How will it help you BE your Best during the next twelve months?

_____

_____

_____

_____

_____

Day 3

"Come near to God and he will come near to you."
James 4:8a

God is all around us. He is in the sunset, a child's laugh, the birds singing, a new job. How can you come near to God today? Where do you see Him, and how can you share your joy with Him?

_____

_____

_____

_____

_____

Day 4

Congratulations! Your hard work and commitment have paid off, and I BElieve you are your BEst self. Spend today reading back through your notes, reflect, and celebrate. Describe what you learned and how your new skills will carry forward to the next twelve months.

_____

_____

_____

_____

_____

Day 5

BrEathe! Congratulate yourself and now the fun. Write your values here, and describe how you will spend the next twelve months living your value system.

_____

_____

_____

_____

_____

May God bless you and keep you and make His face to shine bright upon you.
BE!!!!

NOTES

BE Authentic

Sanders, Jamelle. *The Undeniable Power of Gratitude.* 11/04/17.
https://www.huffingtonpost.com/entry/the-undeniable-power-of-gratitude_us_59fdcc8be4b0d467d4c2254c

Holmes, Lindsay. *10 Things Grateful People Do Differently.* 11/26/2015.
https://www.huffpost.com/entry/habits-of-grateful-people_n_565352a6e4b0d4093a588538

Dweck, Carol. PhD. 2006. *Mindset, the New Psychology of Success.* New York. Ballantine Books.

BE Confident

Peterson, Jordan. 2018. 12 rules for life: An Antidote to Chaos. New York. Penguin Random House.

Batterson, Mark. *In A Pit With A Lion on a Snowy Day.* 2006. Colorado Springs. Multnomah.

Brennan, Bridget. Why Have Women's Economic Power Surged? Five Stats you Need to Know.
1/31/2017. https://www.forbes.com/sites/bridgetbrennan/2017/01/31/why-has-womens-economic-power-surged-five-stats-you-need-to-know

Sullivan, Bob. 2017 State of Credit report by Experian. 1.11.2018. https://www.experian.com/blogs/ask-experian/state-of-credit/

Urist, Jacoba. What the Marshmallow Test really teaches us about self-control. 9.24.2014. https://www.theatlantic.com/health/archive/2014/09/what-the-marshmallow-test-really-teaches-about-self-control/380673/

BE Curious

George Land and Beth Jarman, *Breaking Point and Beyond.* 1993. San Francisco: Harper Business.

Vozza, Stephanie. *8 Habits of Curious People.* 4.21.2015. https://www.fastcompany.com/3045148/8-habits-of-curious-people

Harris. Carla. *Expect to Win: 10 Proven Strategies for Thriving in the Workplace.* 2009. New York. Hudson Street Press.

Tomas Chamorro-Premuzic, Tomas. You Can Teach Someone to be More Creative. 2.23.2015. https://hbr.org/2015/02/you-can-teach-someone-to-be-more-creative

BE Disciplined

Duhigg, Charles. *The Power of Habit. Why We Do What We Do in Life and Business.* 2014. New York. Random House.

Duckworth, Angela. *Grit. The Power of Passion and Perseverance*. 2016. New York. Simon & Schuster, Inc.
Doerr, John. *Measure What Matters*. 2018. New York. Penguin Random House.

McRaven, William, Admiral. *Make Your Bed*. 2017. Hachette Book Group. New York.

BE Encouraging
Rath, Tom. *StrengthFinders 2.0*. 2007. New York. Gallup Press.

BE Faithful
McCarthy, Kevin. *On Purpose Person*. 1992. Colorado Springs. Pinon Press.

Jones, Laurie Beth. *The Path*. 1996. Hyperion. New York.

Anxiety and Depression Association. https://www.tricare-west.com/content/hnfs/home/tw/bene/mentalhealth/anxiety.html

BE Fun
Tenth Leading Causes of Death By Age Group. 2016 https://www.cdc.gov/injury/wisqars/pdf/leading_causes_of_death_by_age_group_2016-508.pdf

Parker-Pope, Tara. The Power OF Positive People. Are your friendships giving you a boost or bringing you down.

7.10.2018. https://www.nytimes.com/2018/07/10/well/
the-power-of-positive-people.html

Macdonald, Cheyenne. *Friendships are more important
than family and can boost our health and happiness as we
age. 6.8.2017. https://www.dailymail.co.uk/sciencetech/
article-4582734/Study-finds-friends-strongly-linked-
happiness.html*

Stillman, Jessica. *Chronic Negativity Can Literally Kill
you Science Shows.* https://www.inc.com/jessica-stillman/
science-the-negative-people-in-your-life-are-literally-
killing-you.html

BE A Goose Leader
AARP Foundation Press Release. 9.25.2018. https://press.
aarp.org/2018-9-25-AARP-Foundation-Survey-Loneli
ness-Numbers-Rise-Among-Adults-Age-45-Older-Neigh
borhood-Connections-Key-Countering-Social-Isolation

Pestano, Aimee Barnes. *10 Characteristics of Truly Strong
Women.* Blog 10.10.2015. https://tangramwellness.com/
blog/2015/10/10/10-characteristics-of-truly-strong-women

Young Entrepreneur Council. *12 Questions to ask your
Mentor ASAP.* https://www.inc.com/young-entrepre-
neur-council/the-12-questions-you-should-be-asking-
your-mentor.html

BE On Purpose
Smartphone market worth $355 billion, with 6 billion devices in circulation by 2020: Report. https://www.cnbc.com/2017/01/17/6-billion-smartphones-will-be-in-circulation-in-2020-ihs-report.html January 17, 2017.

BE Respectful
Covey, Stephen. *The Seven Habits of Highly Successful People. 2013.* New York. Rosetta Books.

Shambora, Jessica. Fortunes' Best Networker. 2.9.2011. http://fortune.com/2011/02/09/fortunes-best-networker/

BE Transformative
https://en.oxforddictionaries.com/definition/advocate

Women in State Legislatures. http://www.cawp.rutgers.edu/women-state-legislature-2017

Corliss, Julie. Mindfulness mediation may ease anxiety, mental stress. 1.8.2014. https://www.health.harvard.edu/blog/mindfulness-meditation-may-ease-anxiety-mental-stress-201401086967

McGreevey, Sue. *Eight weeks to better brain*. 1.21.2011. https://news.harvard.edu/gazette/story/2011/01/eight-weeks-to-a-better-brain/

Talk of the Nation. The Myth of Multitasking. 5.10.2014. https://www.npr.org/2013/05/10/182861382/the-myth-of-multitasking.

Depression: A Global Health Crisis. October 10, 2012. Forward by Deborah Wan. https://www.who.int/mental_health/management/depression/wfmh_paper_depression_wmhd_2012.pdf

Wehrwein, Peter. *Astounding increase in antidepressant use in Americans.* 10.20.2011. https://www.health.harvard.edu/blog/astounding-increase-in-antidepressant-use-by-americans-201110203624

Goldman, Bruce. *Study shows how slow breathing induces tranquility. 3.20.2017.* https://med.stanford.edu/news/all-news/2017/03/study-discovers-how-slow-breathing-induces-tranquility.html.

CPSIA information can be obtained
at www.ICGtesting.com
Printed in the USA
BVHW072154260921
617557BV00002B/11